The Terry Lectures

. .

The Self
Its Body and Freedom

THE SELF
ITS BODY AND FREEDOM

BY

WILLIAM ERNEST HOCKING

NEW HAVEN : YALE UNIVERSITY PRESS

LONDON : HUMPHREY MILFORD

OXFORD UNIVERSITY PRESS

TO

RICHARD CABOT

PHYSICIAN · PHILOSOPHER · FRIEND

PREFACE

PHILOSOPHY is always in danger of being thought of as the special business of its devotees. Its very name seems to assign it a place among the abstractions and technicalities. It thus becomes one of its chief obligations to persuade men that philosophy is every man's business; and that the kingdom of philosophic truth is within them. Especially in the central questions regarding the mind, the body and freedom, mankind is cozened with appalling ease out of its rightful persuasion that we have in our own persons, each one of us, all of the facts.

The mind is not really a foreign body, about which we must learn chiefly through the reports of travelers or laboratory specialists; yet in all ages how docile we have been, and what weird things we have been willing to take ourselves to be! We are breath, shadow, heart, several souls at once, atoms, fire, force . . . ; we are bundles of habits, of instincts, of conditioned responses . . . ; we are ectoplasmic protosubstance; we are conscious and subconscious, a group of complexes; we are repressing censor and repressed impulse, a hostile pair of inner springs. . . . The ancient substitutes for self were comparatively simple. The modern preference is for a little mechanism with a moderate degree of intricacy. In any current psychology it is a point in its favor if after a few lessons one can learn to operate it, with a satisfying sense of initiation. Thus in a busy modern world, the self fathoms the self, together with much other business, in the course of the day's work!

Unquestionably, these inner mechanisms or some such mechanisms exist. Unquestionably, too, man is a mystery to himself, and somehow entertains the mechanisms without being exhausted in or controlled by them. But unquestionably also a genuine self-knowledge is his prerogative and his destiny. A recall to such self-knowledge, the normal and deepening self-knowledge of the race, is one of the perennial functions of philosophy.

In exercising this function, it acts as critic —not of psychology, but of certain aberrations such as spring up abundantly in an era of great psychological advance. It ventures even to contribute to psychology, on the ground of the persuasion referred to, that the truth about the self is not far from any of us, and that here, the technician and the uncommitted observer may fairly assume the existence of a common interest and a common ground.

To contribute in such an untechnical way toward our sense of proportion in psychology is one of the objects sought in these lectures. Their main concern is with the old question, How is the self set in the world of nature? The relatively novel ideas they contain are chiefly ways of gaining advantageous outlooks on truth, the common and ancient truth. These ideas are set in phrases which by deliberate intention recur. It might be well to draw up a list of them here, as a sort of prelude, giving the Leitmotifs of our argument. They will be cabalistic apart from that argument; but they may be read again after it:

> The self is half the world it perceives;
> What my body does, I do;
> Sensation is not from nature, but in nature;
> For mind, space and time may have plurals;
> Meaning descends from a single source;
> The essence of a habit is its meaning;
> To be is to accept being;
> Nature draws consequences;
> Selves may overlap;
> A self is a hope.

WILLIAM ERNEST HOCKING

Madison, New Hampshire,
  August 9, 1927

CONTENTS

I. Two Views of Self   1
   1. What is man?
   2. An official portrait of self
   3. The original versus the portrait

II. "Why the Mind Needs a Body"   51
   4. Cycles of causation
   5. Dualism reconsidered
   6. The body as a member of the self

III. The Self and Nature   99
   7. A servant of two masters
   8. The stranger in the house
   9. Nature the consumer

IV. Freedom   143
   10. Freedom from within
   11. Freedom from without
   12. Degrees of freedom

I.

TWO VIEWS OF SELF

Two Views of Self

1. WHAT IS MAN?

MAN has been said to be the animal that laughs. The distinction is probably safe, though not wholly unassailable. But surely man is the animal that makes pictures.

He has been at it from very early times —witness the aboriginal cave drawings, the carved handles of stone knives and the like. And he is always at it. It expresses a peculiarity of his mind—disinterested thinking. Whoever makes a picture has turned a corner in evolution: he has become so far a mental being that the form of an object is worth something to him without the object. He has an "idea" which is worth keeping; and the visible mark, however rude, aids him to steady that idea before his mind and think about it.

This trait of making pictures seems to me to refute the pragmatic theory that our ideas are essentially instruments of action. It may be that the ideas of animals run out immediately into the muscles; but the pic-

ture is the idea halted in its active course.
It can do nothing more for its owner: it
is there for contemplation and not for em-
bodiment. It turns out, indeed, to have
enormous practical value. The successful
artist enjoys a sense of control over the
form of his object: he feels that he has
taken possession of its essence. The primitive artist is to be excused if he thinks that
his picture gives him magical powers over
the real object. The image of the stag he
cannot catch may be just the charm that
helps him to secure it. But had he been
solely occupied in hunting stags, and had
he never independently drawn pictures, it
would hardly have occurred to him that
making a picture was a promising device
for the hunter. The utility is an afterthought. And so is that far greater utility
in which the picture becomes the precur-
sor of written language and the great instrument of advancing reason. The essence
of the picture is an enjoyment of the meaning of things apart from their changing
aspects: it is the capture of a fragment of
eternity out of the flux of events.

Now at some stage in his growth, man's

pictures begin to appear to him literally as fragments or preliminary sketches for a possible great picture—a picture of the universe. Among the ideas he contemplates there is one idea that haunts him—the idea of the whole. He recognizes that it is implied in all his sketches. In some of the more ambitious attempts of ancient Egyptian, Hindu, and Chinese artists, the gods are seen mingling with men, and the cosmic elements take their places. These world-pictures are philosophies; and all philosophies are world-pictures. But the impulse that leads to making them is religion.

Religion is man's intuition of his destiny to have commerce with the ultimate powers of the world, and the impulse which accompanies that intuition. It nerves him to the audacious effort to match his thought against the whole of things, and to make that whole an object of contemplative enjoyment.

In making this world-picture it becomes necessary to include the human self, the self of the artist and of his fellow beings.

For the mind capable of caring for pictures is also interested in itself; and, of course, few pictures are wholly satisfactory unless one's self is in them—least of all a world-picture; for any philosophy must indicate man's place in the world. Now every artist is at an evident disadvantage in portraying himself; and in the case of the world-view there arises a set of puzzles which it is the particular interest of these lectures to consider. For beside the well-known difficulties of true self-observation, there is the added difficulty that we have *two views* of ourselves, and that these two views seem to disagree.

The first view is that steady awareness of our own being which accompanies our awareness of everything whatever. To see a thing is *to see;* that is, when I look at a thing certain questions about form and color of the thing are being answered, and those questions and answers are so many events in me. Likewise with everything that I handle or think about or in any way deal with: it is there for me, and there is some event in me that corresponds to my knowledge of it. There are as many of these events in me as there are things in the world of which I take account. The self is thus the counterpart of the whole of the observed world: it would not be wholly absurd to say that there is as much of self as there is of the world: ego and non-ego are on a par with each other. As William James once put the case, every individual dichotomizes the universe: in the direct awareness of living, the self is half of the world it perceives.*

It would be more accurate to say that for immediate awareness the self *pervades* its world—fractions are obvious follies and therefore harmless; but the language we have used may suggest well enough the perspective immensity of the self to itself in this first and most intimate view.

The second view is less direct. Among the objects in my world there are some

* There are not a few thinkers who would say that the self includes *all* that it perceives: its objects are its contents. These are the thinkers who consider that for each self the world is ego-centric, and who feel obliged to explain how any self gets knowledge of the world beyond itself. Please note that my estimate is more modest; and that I avoid the ego-centric predicament by limiting the self to a mere half of its presented world.

which I regard as other selves. Each one
of these is but a small fraction of the total
world; their bodies are very minute compared with the total canvas—there is room
for many of them in the picture. But having recognized them as other selves, I
find that, by implication, I have thereby
counted myself as one of them. I am myself; but I am also a member of this class,
the genus homo. And this fact strangely
reduces my proportions; from being com-
mensurate with the whole, I become com-
mensurate with a very small part, a mere
spot in the landscape.

It is hard to unite these two views. And
when I ask myself the reason for the difference between them, I see that it is the
bodies of the others rather than their minds
which give me this impression. As a Mind,
man does not see himself as part of nature,
but *nature is over against him,* as a field
of objects, *his* objects. As a Body, he is a
part of nature. His body acts; but it acts
solely by energies which it derives from
the rest of the world: it is a passageway
through which certain streams of causality
flow, and we may say, if we like, that by

way of the human body nature is acting upon itself.

Let us refer to these two views as the internal view and the external view. Which is the true view? Can both of them be true? If so, how can we unite them? Is one truer or primary while the other is subordinate or out of focus? The answer to these questions is by no means a matter of indifference.

For many reasons the external view, which identifies the human self with the living human body, appears the more valid and definitive. The internal view is primitive and self-centered: the external view is thoughtful and well considered—it corrects the distortions of our self-absorbed perspective. It is scientific; and it is practical. It accords with our well-established habit of locating ourselves by way of our bodies— "Here I am!" It works to treat the body and the self as equivalent: aid the body and you aid the man; arrest the body and you arrest *him;* if you wish to set him free you seek a writ not of *habeas mentem* but of *habeas corpus.* The moral law also sides

with this view: the essence of our duty is
to count ourselves as one and only one, to
get rid of our egoism, to think of ourselves
generically (or as Kant would say, univer-
sally) as members of a group of equals in
the all-inclusive world of nature. And religion adds its admonition not to think of
ourselves more highly than we ought to
think, to love our neighbors as ourselves,
to work for human fraternity. All these interests conspire to reduce the sanguine ex-
pansiveness of selfhood, until it can take
itself as one among many, the mere unit-
spot in the infinite landscape of nature.

But if this external view is the whole
truth, the corollaries are somewhat dis-
turbing. If man is a part of nature, and
nothing in contrast to nature, it would follow as Mr. Bertrand Russell has recently
said, that the laws which govern his conduct are the laws which govern the movements of stars and atoms. In all our do-
ings, in spite of our sense of freedom, we
are doing solely as we must. When the
brain ceases to function the mind ceases to
exist: the notion of a separable soul is an
illusion. As a product of nature, the hu-

man self is the result of two parental elements: it can set up no case for that kind
of atomic simplicity which Plato thought
might ensure its immortality, even if there
were any other world to live in. Man may
indeed have a "higher life" which rescues
him from the mire of exclusive self-inter-
est and self-indulgence: that is his life in
society. But society itself is completely
contained in the domain of physics: with
the death of the planet society must die
also. The career of the race, like the career
of the individual, is enclosed in nature.
Certainly these are sane conclusions, fa-
vored by every visible appearance: indeed
they are so sane and obvious as to be totally
devoid of novelty or intellectual remark,
for they are as ancient as this external view
of man.

What is remarkable is that the race with
singular accord and persistence has declined to accept them. It is an easy fling
to say that it has done so merely on the
ground of its wishes, and in the teeth of all
the evidence. I think it more likely that it
has done so on the ground of a lurking
sense that the first view of self has still to

be considered: we shall not now debate
whether this is so. We shall only point out
that this strange refusal has not been of the
fair-weather variety. It is just those crises
of experience when nature gives the clear-
est demonstration of its capacity to swal-
low man up that man has issued his rejec-
tion of those claims, not simply in the form
of statements of belief, but in the form of
ceremonial institutions, the most persistent and universal products of his early religion. For the major ceremonies of religion
are so many gestures of defiance to the
claim of nature.

What is the most complete and universal assertion of nature's power over man?
Death. What is the most universal and
emphatic of all rites? The burial rite, which
is the ceremonial denial of that assertion.
Marriage is hardly second in this respect—
marriage, the chief of those unreasoned
crises of experience in which the biological
demands of the species assert themselves in
the form of a personal inclination. Psychologically, this inclination is the most private of all interests, the business of no one
in the world beyond the two concerned un-

less and until children come of it. Yet throughout history the public ceremony which interferes has been not endured but sought, as if to reject the suggestion that either the biology or the psychology of marriage is its essential character. Likewise at every other turn of experience where physical exigency tends to insist on man's physical essence and dependence—at birth, in mutilation and the loss of blood, in the need of food, in illness—taboos and ceremonial purifications have grown up to resist these claims. And as for that omnipresent plea of the self-excusing culprit, "I couldn't help it, nature did it"—law, whether sacred or secular, is the universal retort of civilized and savage man. Law as an agreement among men to hold themselves to some things they ought to do is a sort of bondage which implies an assertion of freedom. The subject of human law is not exclusively subject to the laws of stars and atoms.

THESE protests are impressive, but they are not conclusive. They demand the respect due to any great body of racial judg-

ment; but as they stand they suffer from
two weaknesses. They are merely dogmatic; they expostulate without argument.
And they are bare negatives: they deny
that the self is solely a thing of nature, but
they offer no tenable view of what else the
self is.

Their origin, too, is in the pre-scientific
stage. This is not in itself anything against
their truth. But we need to reconsider their
force under the changed light of present
knowledge.

2. AN OFFICIAL PORTRAIT OF SELF

SCIENCE is a child of two parents, disinterested curiosity and the interest in pre-
dicting and controlling events. From both
sides, it is occupied with the conditions
under which events take place, their immediate causes, their historic origins. As
the mind becomes an object of scientific
study, we are bound to consider it as if it
were, like other natural objects, a matter
of cause and effect.

The mind has not resisted this treat-
ment. It cannot be said that the laws of the
stars or the laws of the atoms have yet shed

any light on mental processes. But the laws
of biology have been more fruitful. And
certain laws, like the laws of association,
apply directly to these mental events, and
form the nucleus of a still young but lusty
natural science of psychology. Every year
adds to the evidence of the rootedness of
man in nature, and so tends to confirm the
finality of the external view of self.

On the growing force of the argument
from evolution there is no need to dwell.
To anyone whose mind is open there can
be no doubt not only that the human body
is animal in its ancient origins, but also that
the mind has evolved with the body, and
that the germs of morality itself are dis-
coverable in the behavior of animals. In
studying the quarrels of birds, Wallace
Craig has noticed, especially among pi-
geons, that an angry bird will moderate his
ferocity when it is directed to a member of
his own household or group. This instinctive mitigation of pugnacity, seen in many
human relationships and embodied in that
earliest of moral rules, Thou shalt not kill
thy blood-brother, Craig attributes to an
elementary moral sense. I see no reason to

doubt this view; nor do I doubt that there
are germs of various other moral attitudes,
such as loyalty, courage, self-sacrifice, and
perhaps—as we shall see later—of religion
itself among the traits of animals. From
every salient angle of his being evolution
ties man with silken threads back into the
embroidery of nature.

But it is to psychology that I wish especially to call your attention. For psychology is by name the science of the mind,
and so, as it were, the official portrait-
painter of the human self. It has acquired
a large repute in recent years, especially
in Germany, England, and America, so
much so that as in the case with other
painters of renown, we have some disposition to accept their portrayals as authentic,
even when we ourselves cannot verify the
likeness.

Psychology in its present form is a very
recent science. Plato and Aristotle were
doubtless notable psychologists in their
day—and what they said of the mind was
peculiarly rich in those *verifiable traits,*
without which no psychology can get a
hearing. But modern psychology owes its

rapid development largely to its willingness to learn of the human self through the human body. In the seventeenth century, the science of mind and the sciences of physical nature were still clearly separate. By the middle of the nineteenth century they had come so close that there was an actual overlapping of territory between psychology and physiology; and "the effect of physiology," as Professor Whitehead says, "was to put mind back into nature."* What course in psychology to-day would be considered complete without an account of the physiology of the nervous system? And we must now add an account of the chemistry of the blood, and of the functions of the glands of internal secretion.

But this is to say, is it not, that psychology in speaking of the mind is guided by what we have called the external view, only making more thorough with it than our ordinary observation can do? True, psychology does not speak with a single voice. There is dynamic psychology and purposive psychology, Gestalt psychology

* *Science and the Modern World*, p. 206.

and reaction psychology, Freudian psychology, structural psychology, behavioristic psychology, and various other schools. They produce different portraits of the self. But the composite of them has a distinctly physiological cast; and we may take behaviorism as the pure instance, because it is the extreme instance, of this character.

BEHAVIORISM proceeds on the reasonable assumption that for scientific purposes the mind must be observable; and that what we can observe of each other, in an objective and verifiable way, is our physical conduct. And, conversely, all that we are is in principle observable. I see not only your presence, but looking at your eyes I see your *seeing*. Looking at your attitude I can see your *listening*. Looking at your head bent over your paper, I can see your *reading*. Regarding carefully the many slight changes of color and tension in the finer muscles of your face, I can see your *feeling,* or a significant part of it; for what is a feeling but an incipient change of attitude which has a thousand slight bodily signs?

You say, I may be mistaken: I cannot really see your reading, for I cannot see what goes on in your mind. Lévy-Bruhl tells of a group of savages who saw a white man reading. Their curiosity was aroused: What is the white man doing? Their wise man said, "The white man is curing his eyes." Such mistakes, you say, would be impossible if the behavior were equivalent to the self. But is the difficulty that we cannot see enough of the mind, or that we cannot see enough of the body? If we knew all the physical facts, including the facts of nervous set and brain-event, would it still be true that to any one physical situation there is more than one mental interpretation? Probably not. To every difference in the bodily state, there is presumably some sort of difference in the mental state; and to every mental difference, some brain-difference, if we were keen enough to detect it. What we want, then, is a scientific study of behavior which penetrates beneath the surface of the body to the usually invisible events in the underlying tissues.

A man who is perfectly quiescent to the outer eye may be having a lively run of

ideas. But what is an idea? A primitive
man, as we saw, might have needed the aid
of a picture to keep the idea before his
mind; his idea would have been the rule of
construction of that picture, and we should
have been able by looking on to tell what
his idea was. But we have learned to make
invisible pictures: when we think, *words*
begin to shape themselves in our vocal organs. Royce used to describe an idea as a
plan of action; and one of the types of action our ideas present is this finesse of the
larynx. It was this insight which inspired a
student of mine to define an idea in this
vein: "An idea is an incipient laryngeal ar-
ticulation, supplemented by certain subtle
visceral reverberations." The language is
strong, but the sense is clear.

We are not greatly concerned here with
the wisdom or folly of particular behavior-
isms, but with the principle, which is twofold. First: that there is a complete and
instant expression of every state of mind in
the infinitely delicate and plastic patterns
of the body, as it deals with its natural
environment. Second: that this expression
is the mind for all scientific purposes, as

well as for the purposes of social intercourse. The mind is not a substance: the
mind is what it does—it is what it does in
the world of nature.

The first of these principles is more
readily accepted than the second.* But the
second also, which simply states that the
external view of the self is the true and
definitive view, no longer meets the ancient
resistance. It simply carries to its logical
conclusion our growing sense of the equivalence of body with mind which comes from
increasingly close and friendly observation. We no longer feel the former aver-
sion, for we are no longer on bad terms
with our bodies as sources of sin and ene-
mies of thought. They are our closest and
most permanent companions, as well as our
most useful tools. As they flourish we flourish; we take care of them because we wish
to take care of ourselves. And when they
have exhausted their energies, shall we not
also be ready to rest from our labors in a
perpetual sleep?

* Though generally challenged by dualistic writers,
prominently by Bergson in *Matter and Memory*, whose
position we have still to consider.

IT was once customary to call beliefs of
this kind materialistic, and to refute them
by the simple device of making clear to
ourselves what we mean by mind and what
we mean by body. If the whole physical
world is a system of material particles moving in space, then the human body as a part
of that world must be in the last analysis a
galaxy of very minute pillules in intricate
and enormously rapid motion. But this picture contains nothing of what we mean by
thought, feeling, love or hate: to identify
any state of mind with a state of matter in
motion is the sort of proposition one can
make only when he has renounced the
meaning of words and stopped thinking.
The *ingredients* of the mind—sensations,
ideas, feelings, volitions—are not the ingredients of physical nature. The *relations*
between these mental ingredients are not
the relations between physical ingredients:
as Hume put it, "a moral reflection cannot
be placed on the right or on the left hand of
a passion, nor can a smell or sound be either
of a circular or a square figure."* Then the
laws of mental events, which express rela-

* *Treatise,* Part IV, sect. 5; Green, II, 520.

tions in time, must be quite distinct from
the laws of physical events. The mental
events may run along together with some
series of physical events in the brain: and
there may be some analogy between their
laws. There is a law of "association" among
ideas; there is a law of social "attraction."
But to identify these with any law of physical attraction is to be betrayed by an analogy. Personal affection does not vary with
the distance of the persons, certainly not
with the inverse square: the rules of quantity, the essence of the physical law, are
impertinent in the mental world. Thus materialism became an impossible position
simply by seeing what it meant.

BUT perhaps modern views of the physical
world may escape these difficulties. For if
there is no matter, there can be no materialism in the literal sense. Look at mind
and body as systems of events rather than
as substances, and the differences between
them seem to become tenuous and recon-
cilable. The *ingredients* lose their dis-
parity; for on the ground of action, mind
and body come to identity. *What my body*

as a whole does, that I do. The time is the
same, the deed is the same, the energy is
the same, the *laws* cannot be wholly di-
verse. To Leibniz, the idea of force seemed
a common meeting ground for mind and
body. The modern physicist takes up the
work of Leibniz in this respect, in so far
as he resolves the world of matter in motion into the conception of a world of electrical charges each one of which is an organization of tensions in the whole of space
from a given center. The transformation
of mechanical mass into electrical mass, the
dismissal of the material ether, the ap-
proximation of the whole physical universe
to a set of applied mathematical event-for-
mulae from whose terms every remnant of
physical imagery has been banished—does
not this dematerialization of nature render
the domestication of the mind within it a
relatively conceivable and probable result?
Instead of that conservation of mass, and
the implied eternity of matter, in which we
were formerly taught to believe, it may
well be that the birth of atoms is taking
place before our eyes,* as if matter itself

* If Nernst's interpretation of Kohlhörster's results

were emerging from an immaterial source
of being.

I cannot doubt that the relegation of
former physical absolutes to a position of
"relativity" must have an important effect
upon our philosophy. Much is to be gained
incidentally by the widespread disposition
among physicists to bring their fundamental ideas of measurement, space, time,
etc., into question, even if some of these
questions show, as I suspect, an open-
minded willingness to contemplate non-
sense formerly thought the exclusive attribute of metaphysicians. But whenever
an older absolute is demoted to the level of
a relative, it becomes relative to a new absolute; and the question of philosophical
importance is, What is the nature of the
new absolute? If one physical absolute is
dethroned in favor of another physical absolute the advance of relativity involves no
radical change in our view of the world.
This could occur only if a physical absolute were made relative to some non-physi-

is true, *i.e.*, that the ultra-x-rays indicate the capture of
an electron by a nucleus, and that the chief source of
these rays is in certain regions of the Milky Way.

cal absolute; and I see no sign that this is
involved or intended in recent physical
theory.

If matter is coming into existence from
the immaterial, it is still assumed to appear under definite conditions and discov-
erable laws. The energy that is involved
submits to physical measurement and
transformation. Whatever the relation is
between the energy of the nervous centers
and "mental energy" (and some intimate
relation I am sure there is), it is not a relation with which physics can operate.

So far as our present problem is concerned, the new physics has, I fear, very
little to offer. We have long known that it
is hopeless to approach mind by refining
matter; though this fallacy has been shared
with primitive peoples by many wise heads,
by the Stoics, the theosophists, those who
take wireless transmission as a step toward
telepathy, and many others. We have now
to see that it is equally hopeless to approach mind by way of refining energy or
events. The difficulty is that there is *no set
of intermediate terms between a physical*

event and an idea—whether an idea of that event or of any other event.

It is really no more satisfactory to be a set of events than a set of billiard balls, if these events are completely out of my knowledge, and subject to laws of causation independent of my desires. If I am to be a calculable mesh of physical entities, I have no preference whether I shall be an electric storm or a cloud of dust. The Stoic inclination to think of man as a flame rather than as a clod was a mere prejudice, for in its ultimate nature no physical unit can be either dirty or dull or less delectable than any other; and the same would be true as between the protons and the ancient atoms. If one is to be governed by the laws of the stars, it must be a matter of indifference whether the laws be Newton's or Einstein's.

But if one external view of the self seems to us more nearly adequate than another, that can only be because we have some standard to judge by. And this can only mean that we have a knowledge of self which is independent of that external view.

It is, in truth, impossible to abandon the internal view of self in behalf of the outer. The older refutations of materialism remain valid in principle for the newer forms of naturalism. No physical explanation of the self can alter the fact that *the self is what it appears to itself to be.* Let it be true that the life of self is explained by transformations of energy in the brain: it is still the thing explained, and not the explanation, that concerns us.

3. THE ORIGINAL *VERSUS* THE PORTRAIT

I SUGGEST that we review with some care three of the ways in which the external view of the self, as depicted by its most faithful interpreters, the behaviorists, must fall short as an account of the self.

First, in regard to *space.* The body is spatial, whether for the old physics or for the new: it has relations of distance to objects outside of it; its parts are near or far, above or below each other. This is not true of the mind, or of any mental events. This is the elementary consideration with which every study of mind and body must begin:

it does not cease to be true because it was stated long ago by Descartes or Hume. We must persistently remind ourselves that the thought of a distant object is not a distant thought, nor the thought of a twisted object a twisted thought. But since familiarity in matters of truth breeds a certain anaesthesia, and provokes the anti-suggestible to feats of that kind of originality which consists in entertaining the absurd, we need to probe in novel directions the antithesis between the spatial and the mental.

Let us consider the notion of "all the space there is." This roomy region might be defined as the path of a sphere centered at some given point and expanding without limit in all directions. It might also be defined as the totality of all positions which can be related to a given position by *distance,* or by a continuous line.

It makes no difference for our present argument whether this all-of-space is finite or infinite; at any rate, there is nothing "outside" it, in the sense of being beyond its boundary. For if there were any spatial beyond, that expanding sphere or those

lines of distance would have to enlarge to
include this beyond. But if all-of-space includes all the positions that can be spatially
related to each other, nothing (other than
these positions) can be spatially related to
all-of-space itself. Hence the *thought* of
all-of-space is not spatially related to it:
it is neither inside it nor outside it nor coincident in extent with it.

Now the mind is capable of thinking not
only of all-of-space, but also of *more than
one* such space-total, as, let us say, the
space of waking hours and the space of
some dream. These two spaces are not
"outside of" each other; for this could only
mean that they were different regions in
the same space. They are not spatially related to each other at all: for there is no line
of distance between any point of one and
any point of the other. The bear of the
dream is not a mile from the bedpost nor
ten feet from the bedpost, nor any other
distance: the question how far he is from
the bed is meaningless, for he is simply not
in the same world. From the standpoint
of space, *another* space is a plain impossi-
bility, for any space contains "all the room

there is." But from the standpoint of
the mind there are many possible space-
worlds, each of which is complete, no one of
which interferes in the least with any other.
Plural spaces are related only *via* the self.
The relation of the self to its space-worlds
is thus not a spatial relation.

To a given body, there is but one space;
to a given mind there are many possible
spaces. The mind is therefore not wholly
representable in the body. The mind, we
may say, is *space-free* as the body is not.

Second, in regard to *time*. Both mental
events and physical events are "in time," in
the sense that they can be before or after or
simultaneous with each other. And every
event, whether of mind or body, must *take
time:* it cannot exist at an instant, for an
instant is merely an abstract cross-section
of an event-duration. An instantaneous
event is no event at all.

But the time-span of a physical event
and the time-span of a mental event are
two radically different things. The time-
span of a physical event is, as it were, all
in the present: it is just that limiting dura-

tion necessary to give meaning to its "direction," its "acceleration," and such other aspects of change as require time to exist. In particular, it is *not cumulative*. The physical event bears all the traces of its history; but it bears them as the rocks bear the traces of their formation, or as the bent spring bears the traces of its tension. These traces are all present facts, and there is no true memory in matter, for there is no real retention of a past. The mind has not only a time-span, but its duration accumulates before it; and, ideally, it has its whole history in its field of time-vision.

Here I am glad to find myself in agreement with Professor Sheldon: and this agreement is all the more welcome, because I am here regretfully parting company with the view that the principle of memory may be traced to the roots of the physical world. Now it is precisely in the physical field that a *perfect recurrence* is conceivable. A frictionless pendulum swinging in an otherwise changeless world would exactly repeat its swing forever; and neither man nor god could tell by any trace in the present swing how many swings had gone before it. For if we are dealing with a perfectly simple process, time leaves no tale: nothing wears out, the energy is forever the same, forever fresh as on the first day, it can show no fatigue and no age.

Die unbegreiflich *kleinen* Werke
Sind herrlich wie am ersten Tag.

As theoretical physicists, indeed, we should have no choice but to assign any such system of recurrent motions an infinite age, if it is a truly self-enclosed system; and to infinite age, age has no meaning.

If there are such things as simple physical elements, they can bear *no sign of time;* for a sign of time is a complication. A growing record carried with one is a growing complication. It is plainly contradictory to the very notion of a physical element.

The brain is a complex part of nature, perhaps the most complex. It has in high degree that kind of complexity we call plasticity: it is capable of bearing present traces of past events in almost limitless profusion. And there is probably some peculiar mark in the brain which distin-

guishes a memory, dated backward, from
an anticipation of the same thing, dated
forward, and from a very faint perception
of the same thing, dated now. But this
mark remains a present mark. It is a *sign*
of pastness; but it is not pastness. The
translation of such marks into true time-
distance remains the prerogative of the
mind; for the mind alone, distinguishing
between genuine pastness and all conceivable present marks of pastness, has a grasp
of the past in its own nature along with
the present and the future.

In still another way, the mind has a peculiar relation to time. Its events may lie
in *more than one* time-order. The ab-
stracted reader of history may be said to
be living in the past; but his thoughts are
still in the same time-order with the present, for if we take "all the time there is,"
past and present, we shall sweep his historical position into our net. But the ab-
stracted reader of fairy tale or allegory or
fable, though placing himself at "once
upon a time," as, let us say, in *Pilgrim's
Progress,* is in an independent time-order:
there is no time-interval between those

events and our own. And while the mind
can never escape the Now of present time
—and thus is never as disengaged from
this-time as from this-space—it is capable,
as the body is not, of inhabiting a plu-
rality of time-orders at once. In this sense,
the mind is *time-free,* as the body is not
time-free.

I WILL mention at present only one other
of these points of difference, though this
one point is perhaps the whole point! That
is that the body is a set of *facts,* and the
mind a set of *meanings.* This states the case
too crudely, but we can now remedy that
defect.

In Thomas Hardy's story, *The Return
of the Native,* much is made of various sig-
nals such as, from time immemorial, lovers,
warriors and criminals have used to create
a private language of their own. A slight
splash is heard in a nearby pool at mid-
night. A small boy reports that a frog has
jumped into the water. To the waiting
maiden, the sound had a wholly different
meaning. She contrives the disappearance
of the small boy, and goes to her appointed

tryst. Now the bodily facts are very much
the same for the boy and for the maid.
They consist of an auditory disturbance
which is referred by both to a familiar
cause—some small object falling into the
water. But here the interpretations di-
verge: to the boy the sound means a frog,
to the maid it means a pebble. In the behavior of the frog the boy has seen nothing
to excite further enquiry. In the behavior
of the pebble, the maid recognizes human
intention, and the answer to certain anx-
ious questions regarding her lover's delay.
To her this trifling sound has a critical
meaning for a whole world of interests
completely out of the boy's ken, such as
triumph over her rival; and it means in ad-
dition a summons for her instant action on
behalf of those interests.

Now shall we say that these various
meanings exist in the mind only, and not
at all in the body? That would hardly be
true. For if the noise means to the boy a
startled frog or to the maid a falling pebble, this implies that the part of the brain
which is affected by the sound is *connected*
with that part which has previously been

affected by the sights of these other events. To physiology, a meaning is simply a connection whereby a disturbance in one center spreads to another.* It is, in one peculiarly turbid phrase, the "condition" of a "conditioned response." A concerted signal establishes an artificial connection; and there is nothing physiologically mysterious, therefore, in the circumstance that a simple sound should, by way of such a bridge, spread far through the brain and initiate disturbances throughout the organism and in its visible behavior. The brain is the organ of such connections, and to this extent it is the organ of meaning: it would thus be far from true to say that meaning is not represented in the body.

But it would be quite true to say that it is *only represented,* and not there in person. A brain-connection is a connection and not a meaning. It only becomes equivalent to a meaning when there is some person present to read it as a meaning. A log fallen across a stream may mean life and freedom to someone trying to escape that

* This is the answer to the telegram puzzle, McDougall, *Body and Mind,* p. 268.

way; but in itself it is just a log across a stream. Brain-connections *mean* something only if there is some *meaner* in the offing. Meaning is like light: when it exists anywhere, everything takes on color as if it owned that color in its own right. As a physical entity, the body is completely devoid of meaning; in the light of the self every atom of it is athrill with significance. But it is only a self that can have or confer or read genuine meanings.*

The plain truth is that the second view of self *means nothing without the first*. It is because we are always taking the internal view for granted that we give so much

---

* The word "meaning" has a twofold use. A *thing* has meaning *for me* when it plays a part in any need or interest of mine. *I* have a meaning when I have an intention or purpose: "I mean to buy a farm." The former use of meaning is evidently due to the latter. If I mean to buy a farm, whatever pertains to farms acquires interest to me. Unless the self means something, things could have no meaning for it.

The mind is always meaning, and there is always for it a *total of meaning,* vague in outline, toward which it bears. Driesch's effort to express meaning psychologically by means of "accents" belonging to each content of consciousness seems to me to lose sight of this essential wholeness. His plea for meaning is of the first importance.

credit to the external view. With the inherent prodigality of the self we are literally giving ourselves away. Behaviorism could not live a moment as psychology were it not for the borrowed capital of conscious meaning. With that capital it can reflect a great amount of light on many obscure and quasi-mechanical processes of the mind. As a method of research the study of behavior can never be dispensed with; no sane psychologist of to-day pretends to get on without it. But when it assumes the airs of an "ism" and claims exclusiveness and self-sufficiency, then it behooves the common sense of mankind to remind it of its sources.

THERE are two points in particular in which the attempt to get on in psychology without reference to the internal view of self seems to me to lead to serious misinterpretations of life. The first of these is in the account of *habit*.

Nothing seems so physical as habit. To do a thing over and over again is to get the habit of doing it, as by a sort of mechanical registration. It is like wearing a

rut in a road. But what habit am I forming? Some years ago, I saw a middle-aged
man flying kites in a field. He did this
several days in succession. He seemed to
be forming the habit of flying kites. On
questioning him I found that he was experimenting with certain problems in
aeronautics. He was not forming a habit
of flying kites, but a habit of working with
these intricate questions. The next week he
spent in bending over a set of drawings.
He was confirming his habit, but in a
wholly different sort of behavior. The habit
you form has to be defined by what you
mean to be doing; and nobody can tell
solely from your behavior what that is. No
doubt there is a purely mechanical momentum acquired by repeated physical action,
but that never constitutes a habit except
by the consent of the owner. If crawling
simply created a habit of crawling, it might
effectively interfere with learning to walk.
But crawling means to the crawler *locomo-
tion,* as a route to all sorts of valuable ends;
and because it has this more liberal meaning, a better way can always drive a worse
into oblivion. What habit an action is

forming depends on what that action
means, and not on its physical description
alone.

The second point in which behaviorism
conspicuously fails is in respect to those
important results which sometimes gather
about the *absence* of being or doing.

If a man acts, he forms habits: but what
if he does not act? Then for behaviorism
there is a simple absence of habit forming.
But there is a difference between forming
no habits, and forming the *habit of doing
nothing;* and the trouble with doing nothing is that one does form the habit of it.
Behaviorism is surely at a disadvantage
to account for this. A good machine may
(in theory) be left idle indefinitely, and
be as ready to start action again as when
it was left; the golf-clubs left in a corner
and the guns standing in the rack are not
becoming indolent of temper. Non-being
can only acquire meaning when there is a
meaning-total which renders the void significant. For the eye which sees a total
field, absence of light becomes one of the
colors. For the mind which presents to itself an achievable total of possible doing,

non-action becomes a significant deed and
establishes its habit. It is only for the conscious self that non-being acquires meaning.

We have hardly begun to recognize the
large personal and social rôle which these
privative meanings play. An aristocracy
built on leisure may produce a type of man
excellent except for what he has the habit
of not doing. What a college education is
worth depends in part on what the student
is failing to do. The fact that during these
years he is not, as a rule, earning his living
as are his fellows of the same age is significant. It may do him no harm; for he may
be fully alive to the social price of what he
accepts. But he may also take on the habit
of alienation from the earning-attitude;
and this is a debit against the worth of college. It is a debit which is likely to count
most heavily in the case of the most amiable
and friendly in temperament, for they are
also gaining the habit of expecting easy
victories. The same principle explains the
self-complacency with which men generally
regard themselves no matter what their degree of villainy; for the positive part of

the conscious life is predominantly respect-
able. The average criminal is a very decent
fellow to talk to, and feels himself to be
such. He encourages the philanthropic illusion. It is the invisible habits of non-
effort, non-resistance, non-endurance and
the like which constitute for him, and for
us also, the sinister element. The rascal in
us does not usually feel himself to be a
rascal; and yet, because of that dimly present total of possible meaning, he *knows*
himself to be one! Conscience is largely
occupied with that which, in terms of behavior, is simply non-existent. And conversely, behaviorism on its own ground can
produce but a crippled account of conscience, if it produces any account at all.

BEING in themselves devoid of meaning,
physical events lack in particular that kind
of intrinsic meaning we call *value*. The
world with which physics deals enjoys
nothing, plans nothing, pursues nothing:
it does solely what it must, without joy, but
also without pain; without hope, but also
without regret or suffering.

And lacking value, it is devoid of moral

quality. Such a world must be, as Professor Hoernlé puts it, *morally neutral*. The acts of nature are neither right nor wrong. The acts of animals we take for the most part as acts of nature. And man also—in so far as he is a thing of nature, his acts are what they must be: the words vice and virtue are sounds without sense. The criminal may reasonably be treated as a patient, an organism to be repaired and reset, but never as a subject of moral reform, never as an object of moral indignation. The truly emancipated mind would have overcome the weaknesses of moral praise and blame. Mr. Bertrand Russell would seem to recommend this attitude, as a corollary from his view of human nature; but I am glad to note that his own mind is not in this respect perfectly emancipated: for it appears that he continues to feel indignation toward those who continue to feel it!

In fact, for a man moral neutrality is an impossible attitude. Man is neutral about nothing. He can never dismiss that motive of disinterested resentment which has sustained the greatest efforts of the race in the name of justice; and which has

still a world of work to do, both in war time
and in times of peace.

The moral indifference of the sun and
the rain is one thing. A divine comprehen-
siveness of sympathy, which would send
the sun and the rain alike on the just and
on the unjust, is another thing, and at the
polar opposite from this state of natural
neutrality.

WE recur to our positive proposition, that
the word self must mean to us what we
know the self to be. In regard to psychology, more than to any other science,
mankind has profound concern in its first
principles, and certain inalienable rights in
regard to the resulting portrait, which is,
after all, its own. It is the more important
that these rights be honestly exercised,
since there is a deep tendency in human
nature to *become like* that which we im-
agine ourselves to be. It is not a matter of
indifference if a human being accepts an
account of himself in terms devoid of
meaning, of value, of purpose and of conscience.

BUT what is it, then, that we are most centrally aware of as ourselves? Is it not the active sense of present well-being and ill-being, pleasure and pain, good and evil, and of a *possible better* toward which we strive?

The self is indeed a system of behavior. But it is a system of *purposive behavior emerging from a persistent hope.* The kernel of the self is its hope. All the good one discovers in experience contributes to the color of that hope; and that hope, in turn, becomes the object of all action. *Meaning descends from this single source* upon the details of behavior.

Now a hope is a hold on a good which is not actual, but only possible. Our life is sustained from moment to moment in part by the good that we enjoy; in part by the belief that a possible good, whose quality we recognize without defining it in clear terms, is destined for us. The object of this hope simply cannot be discovered in the present world of facts. The possible is not the actual; the value is not the bare fact: hence the essence of selfhood is doubly indiscoverable in the field of reaction-experiments, conditioned responses, and curves of learning.

THIS is not merely another negative conclusion. Yet it may leave us where Descartes was left, with the conviction that the mind is one thing and the body another; and that the course of wisdom is to recognize the alienness of their natures and the mystery of their union. This is the position of *dualism;* and there are many distinguished thinkers of the present day who are inclining toward it, because of just such impossibilities of a physical psychology as we have been reviewing. Bergson, in *Matter and Memory,* chiefly interested in the relation of the mind to time, may be regarded as the leader of this movement. Driesch, McDougall and Pratt, each on his own ground, have reached a similar conclusion. Lord Balfour has recently expressed the opinion that a dualistic picture of the world is the best we can make at present, though, he adds, mind and matter "remain in contact along a common frontier."

But that common frontier is the obsta-

cle: for a frontier is a line between entities
of much the same sort. The completeness
with which Descartes separated mind and
body was his own undoing; for he was then
obliged to bring them together, and his
effort to do so—on this point, please note,
philosophers are almost unanimous!—was
one of the most brilliant speculative fail-
ures of history. The mind *is* a system of
behavior; and what the body as a whole
does, *I do*.*

The relation between mind and body
can in no sense be accidental; neither can
it be one of essential independence, still
less of opposition. And it is fair to recall
that religion has commonly insisted as
much on the union of soul and body as on
their contrast. The soul could leave *this*
body, but it needed a body of its own. And
some effort was made, as in Egypt and in
Christian tradition to secure to it the use of
its own body in another life. There is a
mediaeval point of view according to which

---

* The phrase "as a whole" is obviously needed to exclude intra-organic processes, digestion, heart-beating,
regulations of a thousand sorts, which cannot be cred-
ited to my conscious self.

the soul when released from its body is discontented until they are rejoined. Miguel de Unamono quotes a Spanish Brother to this effect:

> They lament in heaven, says our Brother Pedro Malón de Chaide, and this lament springs from their not being perfectly whole in heaven, for *only the soul is there* . . . they are therefore not wholly content: they will be so when they are clothed with their own bodies.*

If we try to identify the mind and the body, we find we must set them apart. If we try to separate them, we must rejoin them. The solution must be found by retaining our sense of the difference between these two objects, and yet recognizing that they belong together in a single system. What that system is I shall now try to indicate.

* *The Tragic Sense of Life,* p. 66. I have condensed the passage, and the italics are mine. I owe the reference to my friend, Rosalind Greene.

II.

"WHY THE MIND NEEDS A BODY"

4. CYCLES OF CAUSATION

DISTINCTIONS are necessary; but dualisms are delusive. The discovery of radical differences between mind and body, whether made by primitive religion or by modern philosophy, solves no problems. In a sense, it is the problem itself. For mind and body come to identity on the ground of action.

On the other hand, we dare not indulge in any short-cuts to monism. It would be easy to reflect that if mind and body are one thing, and if that thing cannot be body, nor any meaningless neutral stuff, it must be mind. The conclusion may be correct, but it is unilluminating.* We want to know

* The trouble with referring everything forthwith to mind is its incorrigible finality, its infertility in explanation. If dualisms are delusive, finalities are unprofitable, and drive the pragmatic thinker back into the juicier inaccuracies of dualism or behaviorism. "Of what use is it," he argues, "to say that value is value and not fact? It is an axiom, if you like, but it throws no light on the nature of value. I seem to understand my pleasures and pains better when I refer them to positive and negative responses; a 'good' is an object toward which I experience an impulse of approach; an 'evil,' one toward which I feel an impulse of recession. If I think of an

how mind and body are united; and to
learn this we must start from the clearly
recognized fact of their difference. A pro-
spective monist must be a *provisional dualist*.

I strongly suspect that the wiser dualists
are also provisional dualists; for they fore-
see the necessity of making their two entities into a system. Balfour speaks of
dualism as merely the best way of assem-
bling our present insight: Bergson tried,
in his Creative Evolution, to derive life and
matter from a single source; Pratt's "dualism of process" looks toward a working
union. These are all wise, and therefore
provisional, dualists. We shall begin with
a provisional dualism.

IN taking this position, we forgo one of
the great assets of behaviorism, its theoretical neatness. It avoids all the puzzles of
interaction between mind and body. Be-

'interest' as a specific neutral pattern correlated with a
peculiar visceral tension which seeks release, that may
not be final, but I can operate with it. In this sense it
explains." The pragmatic interest is valid: thinkers must
not be put to the impossible choice between truth and
the usable or fertile hypothesis.

havior is a physical fact; and for physical facts, the physiologist need look for none but physical causes. In tracing the muscular movement back through the nerves to the brain and thence to the stimulus he never discovers the intrusion of an invisible factor called consciousness, and he never feels the need of it. In Professor Whitehead's phrase, when we observe nature it appears "closed to mind": when we adjust our eyes to the external view, the internal view is simply out of focus, and the external view appears to be complete and seamless.

We forego this theoretical clean-cutness: we cannot begin with a false identification of mind and body. We must face, then, the dilemma of the dualist, namely this: If the mind and the body are different, they either affect each other or they do not; and whether we take one alternative or the other, we meet difficulty. Suppose they do not affect each other: suppose the mind keeps to its own world, and its changes or events run along parallel with changes in the body according to some principle of non-interference and harmony. Then we must say that the mind, being without effect on the body, is a wholly useless and ineffectual outrider of the events of nature, witnessing but not literally "doing" anything that occurs there, not even the deeds of its own body-muscles. Suppose, however, that they do affect each other; that the mind works on the body and the body on the mind. Then we intrude into the otherwise regular and cleanly physical processes of nature certain mental factors which are intangible and incalculable; and we are quite at a loss to point out how and where these supposed interactions take place. For no one ever perceives the mind in the act of affecting the body, nor the body affecting the mind; on this crucial point of the theory, there are *no observable facts*.

In this predicament, let us assume the second alternative as our tentative hypothesis. For the mind-body system, whatever it is, is not of an idle or let-alone or merely mirroring variety: it is a system in which each has its function. I am willing to take it as an axiom of my study that conscious purpose cannot possibly be a negligible and ineffective accident in the life of the human organism. In the act of distinguishing mind and body, we define objects which do affect one another. If we cannot find the point of contact and the manner, we are not worse off than in many other admittedly causal sequences: if we limit the meaning of causation to the prevailing scientific view, that of the regular succession of appropriate antecedents and consequents, we need not hesitate to say that body-changes commonly cause mind-changes, and mind-changes commonly cause body-changes. Let us see how this hypothesis works out.

IF mind affects body and body affects mind, there is a certain symmetry and equivalence in their agency. Either or neither may be regarded as the first cause. It may be that a body-change first causes a mind-change, and then the mind-change causes the body-change; in this case, the body is simply changing itself by way of the mind as an instrument. The body makes me thirsty; then my thirst leads me to get a drink; and so my body has re-

plenished its water-supply by making use
of my consciousness. Or it may be that
the mind first effects body-change, and
the body-change then produces a mind-
change; in which case, the mind is altering
itself by way of the body. Thus, I feel dull
in the morning and so put a cup of coffee
into the body-machine and find my slug-
gish thought-activity stirred up. In these
cycles which is the true origin of causation? The facts which chiefly concern us
are those which bear on this question of
originality of causation; and it is for this
reason that the physiological facts relating
to character and emotion have attained
such notoriety.

There is not the slightest reason to doubt
the broad fact of the profound effect on
temperament exercised by the glands of
internal secretion, such as the thyroid or
the interstitial glands or the adrenals. The
stimulation of certain of these glands, or
the injection of their products, or feeding
therewith, may produce changes which
would once have been thought miraculous.
By administering thyroxin a cretin may
be brought to something resembling nor-

mality; if the dosage is stopped he returns to his original condition. If the dosage is increased, unfortunately, neither he nor anyone is raised from normality to genius; we only produce another form of abnormality. And so far, no chemical discoveries justify any bright hopes of improving the human normal. There are, indeed, certain drugs which make an individual feel like a genius, but unless the results are judged under the same influence they are strangely disappointing. We must, therefore, not build at once too high hopes for the future of mankind on these discoveries. But there is a genuine sense in which the soul has its chemistry, and "a deficiency of iodine will turn a clever man into an idiot."

The novel element in these facts is that this sensitive chemical regulation of the mind is internal. Otherwise the principle is not new. It is only recently that we have known that a deficiency of iodine will turn a clever man into an idiot; but we have long known the still more remarkable fact that a deficiency of oxygen will turn a live man into a dead one. This knowledge carried with it the concern of a live man to avoid having a deficiency of oxygen: it now becomes the business of a clever man to avoid having a deficiency of iodine. In brief, neither the new facts nor the old determine whether their rôle is to bring the mind under the control of the body, or to bring the mind under its own control by way of the body. To get light on this question, let us examine somewhat more minutely the physiology of the emotions.

THE well-known theory of emotion attributed to James and Lange holds that the apparent bodily effects of an emotion are in reality part of the cause. It is not that we cry because we are sorry, but that we are sorry because we cry; we are gay because we laugh; we are courageous because we hold our head high, throw a chest, step out boldly, and if need be, whistle. Everybody knows these effects; the theory would have gained no celebrity if it had no support in experience. Hearing himself weep is often the first convincing proof a child has that he is in trouble. I have a gentle friend of saintly character who testifies that the process of chopping wood makes her actually angry, not because she does not like it, but because the attack on the wood so closely dramatizes pugnacity.

Now the chemistry of the soul supplements these facts. An emotion expresses itself not alone in the muscles, but throughout the body, in altered respiration and heartbeat, in increased secretion of these endocrine glands. May we not produce the emotion by bringing about these internal changes as well as by enacting the muscular picture of emotion? The adrenal secretion is used in medicine, and several observers have noticed that the use of it may have certain emotional effects. Dr. G. Marañon of Madrid has found that in some persons the injection of adrenin into the blood will, without any other apparent cause, be followed by feelings of dread or elation or other emotion.

It has also been shown* that any intense muscular action tends to bring about increased adrenal secretion. This fact aids us to see what happens when we simulate an emotion. The muscular activity (as of

* Hartmann, Waite, and Powell, *American Journal of Physiology,* 1922, p. 255.

chopping wood) brings about the adrenal
flow and the various visceral changes which
follow the altered composition of the blood.
Thus the bodily aspect of the emotion is
completed, and the putting on of an emotional expression brings the emotion in
train as its effect. The process seems to run
from the body to the mind.

But the facts are not yet all before us.
We have to remember that Dr. Cannon's
famous experiments began with the mind.
He produced actual fear and rage; and it
was these which brought about the increased adrenal secretion, and therewith
the whole series of visceral changes, preparing the organism for the heavy activities of flight or combat. When Dr.
Marañon found that the injection of adrenin tended to bring about a disturbed state
of feeling in certain sensitive patients he
noted that in most cases what occurred was
not a real emotion, but only as it were an
actor's picture of the emotion which the
patient observed as a cold outsider, *en
froid*. Unless the patient were predisposed
(as by some recent actual occasion for

grief) to be moved, he reported his feelings
with the phrase "as if": "I feel as if I were
afraid" or "as if I expected great joy," or
"as if I were going to cry without knowing
why." The physical aspect, or as Marañon
calls it, the vegetative aspect of the emotion occurs without the emotion. These
facts radically alter our reading of the
body-mind situation.

To Dr. Marañon they furnish a "complete disproof" of the James-Lange theory. For they show that the flow of causation from the bodily expression to the
mental effect is irregular and imperfect.
And the comparative infrequency of
marked emotional effects in a drug so
widely used emphasizes the point that this
direction of causation from the outward
to the inward is exceptional. It is as if it
were, in the order of nature, *part* of a total
phenomenon, and quite embarrassed at
trying to be the whole of it!

These conclusions are reënforced by still
other facts brought to light by more recent
experiments of Cannon and Britton. They
enable us to complete a picture of the nor-

mal order of development of an emotion,* as follows:

1. The exciting idea in the mind;
2. Beginnings of disturbance in skeletal muscles and viscera, with increased adrenal flow;
3. The mind becomes aware of these changes (an incipient James-Lange effect);
4. The mind consents, or does not consent, to the further development of these expressive changes in the muscles under its control. Then, if consent is given;
5. Increased muscular activity and increased adrenal secretion;
6. Mental awareness of these changes (full James-Lange effect);
7. Development and exhaustion of the emotion.

This order of events falls into two cycles. The first (1-3) is preliminary. The second (4-7) is the full-fledged emotion. The mind's initiative appears at two points, at 1 and at 4. It is to this point 4, which is critical for the development of the emotion, that I wish particularly to draw attention. This point we may call the *threshold of*

* I must not make the authors whose data I am relying on responsible for this arrangement. It is my own way of reconstructing the facts they have brought to light. See their report on "Pseudaffective Medulliad-renal Secretion," *American Journal of Physiology,* 1925, p. 283.

consent; for if the activities of the skeletal muscles are not consented to, the emotion does not develop. This corresponds with what we know of the growth of emotion in ourselves. In the first phase of wrath, we stand as onlookers—we feel our choler rising: there is a moment in which we seem aware that it depends on our consent whether the feeling grows to the point of passion. If at this stage we follow the old advice and "count ten," what we do is to enlarge the threshold, and give competing thoughts a chance to be heard.

This threshold of consent is an important possession. Dr. Cannon calls attention to it at the close of his study, and suggests that here the issue appears to be raised how deeply the emotion shall involve the organism.* The function of the self, if consent is

* "The interesting question is raised whether inhibition of the somatic expressions of emotional disturbance may not be accompanied by a correspondingly smaller expression of the visceral functions. The control of one's behavior when there is danger that expression may be excessive may have more than superficial effects," *op. cit.,* p. 293. This conjecture is confirmed by later experiments. Cannon and Britton, "The Influence of Motion and Emotion on Medulliadrenal Secretion," *American Journal of Physiology,* January, 1927, esp. p. 462.

not given, may be described as "control"
or "restraint," but not as *"repression"*: it
is simply determining whether there shall
be a full-grown emotional impulse to repress. It appears to lie in the individual's
control, at this point, whether he allows his
feeling to reach that stage of insistence *at
which what the Freudians call repression
is either necessary or possible.*

The Freudian doctrine of repression is
based on two assumptions. First, that the
strength or force of our impulses is a given
fact with which our conscious selves have
nothing to do. Second, that if impulses are
repressed they or their energies continue
to exist in subconsciousness, finding irregular outlets as in dreams, and working
mischief with mental health.

In view of the facts we have been reviewing, the first assumption is false. How
strong any impulse is depends on how far
we encourage it to grow. The problem of
the expression or repression of sex-im-
pulses, in particular, demands a radically
different statement from that which the
Freudians give it. For unless one has been
a consenting factor in the early stages of

these impulses, they need never acquire that organic momentum at which the problem of repression becomes acute and perilous. Purveyors of psycho-analytic cures, by luring these impulses to the surface, are likely to develop what is healthily latent and thus cause the disease for which they profess to offer a remedy. The thesis that a repression dangerous for mental stability is a necessary and general accompaniment of such a social order as our own has no scientific leg to stand on.

And the confusion of repression with restraint or control reaches the dimensions of a social and educational humbug. Civilization is dependent for its existence not on repression but on the restraint of random impulses, and especially on three restraints—that of the random fight-impulse in the interest of orderly living, that of the random sex-impulse in the interest of the family, that of the random grab-impulse in the interest of property. According to the wise Julius Lippert these three restraints have already become "secondary instincts" and to break them down does violence to nature itself. The distinctive thing about human nature is not its gush, but its *balance;* and balance implies a harmony of restraints.

WHAT is true of the development of emotion is simply a special case of all our mental dealings with the outer world. Except in the simplest reflexes, like winking, no stimulus has all its own mechanical way with us. It depends on us which of the thousands of appeals raining upon our sense-organs every moment we shall attend to; that is, it depends on us whether they shall become "stimuli" or not. I am dimly aware of wild birds flying northward, and spring is invading the air, but if other goods hold the stage, they may fail to strike as deep as the center of action, and so never attain the dignity of stimuli. If I let my attention wander that way, that strange ancient Wanderlust may stir all my members and compel another decision. Our response to outer things is thus "circular," and the self stands at the head of the cycle.

This is especially visible in the case of *new* allurements. We have seen children gingerly and skeptically tasting a new dish which they have been assured is good. They are making use of their threshold of consent. We all find our way into new regions of experience by way of such tentative sampling—of new mental and moral goods as well as of new physical goods. We know that they may become *causes* of which we must entertain the effects; and we propose to *decide whether they shall become causes or not.* Thus, we have heard it said that courage is a good thing, but we have never tried it. Some day we invest a small amount in courage, and find it invites us to further trials. One makes his first speech, let us say, and finds to his surprise that he is listened to: he thereupon continues to speak with greater assurance, and so breaks his way into a new power. He says, as the feeling of capacity mounts in him: "This way to myself!" The process is circular. Many men have failed to attain leadership because they have never made the first venture which throws those about them into the attitude of followers and so redoubles the effect of their suggestions. Some adventurous spirits take to a new experience with a great dive and splash:

they then have much to enjoy, or much to reject. Others move into the untried with a painful cautiousness. But all go forward with the experimental intent and self-reservation. Never without this preliminary consent is the self a direct mechanical effect of physical causes, a response to stimuli. By its threshold of consent it becomes at least the permissive cause of its causes, and so the indirect cause of itself.

We have been dealing with the circular responses of the normal mental life. There are abnormal circles as well. Any physical disease is likely to involve the mind. The diseased mind will react unfavorably on the progress of the disease. A dyspepsia may induce mental gloom, and this lack of cheer may still further diminish the forces that are trying to deal with the digestive problem. A disease tends to establish a vicious circle of this sort.

The cure of the disease requires the breaking of this vicious circle. It may be broken in the body, by medicine or the recovery of bodily balance. It may also be broken in the mind. There is no good reason why a thoroughly vicious circle should not be attacked in as many points as possible. It is foolish not to use medicine if there is a medicine which will help the distracted body. It is equally foolish not to attack it also in the mind. Psychotherapy is becoming a recognized part of the regular practice of medicine. It has always been an important part of this practice; for the mere presence of the physician, as one who knows what is to be done, and who is calm in the emergency, is the beginning of psychotherapy. It is well to note that the force of this reassuring effect depends on the physician's knowledge of disease. The friend who with all good will merely slaps my shoulder and says, "Cheer up, old fellow, you'll be all right," has no such weight. Nor have I, when I tell myself the same story!

When Berkeley had published his *Principles of Human Knowledge,* his system of idealism, which was rumored to turn things into "ideas," springing at once into fame, had also to run the gauntlet of ridicule. His physician wrote to Dean Swift on one occasion that it had been going ill with poor Berkeley. For, he said, "he has had the *idea* of a fever so strong on him that it has been hard to induce in him the contrary *idea* of health." He was describing more accurately than he knew a part of his duty as a physician. And we are not to think that the mind attends merely to its own part of the vicious circle, while the body independently works out its own cure. For it is evident, in many cases, that the mind has the very chemistry of the body to some extent under its control. Dr. Richard Cabot has recently described a case reported from the Cook County Hospital in Chicago in which the knitting of the bone of a broken leg depended on discovering and removing a persistent anxiety of the patient. As he explains the situation, the patient

did not know whether he, the principal breadwinner, was being missed by his family at home to the extent of serious want. Because of that uncertainty he was losing sleep; because of losing sleep he was losing appetite; because he was losing appetite he was losing nutrition; and because nutrition was not going on as it should, those chemical and physical changes which unite a bone when it is broken were not taking place.*

* *Harvard Alumni Bulletin,* December, 1925, p. 386.

When he was informed that all was well with his family, the bone began to knit. This is only a particularly organic instance of what we all know of the effect of "morale" in bracing all the circuits of the body and multiplying all the available "energies of men." In such cases, the initiation of the critical changes seems to lie with the mind.

I say "seems to lie," for physical concomitants can be found or assumed for every state of mind, including these acts which appear to us as movements of initiative. But there are certain rough and ready, if not conclusive, reasons for accepting this appearance of mental initiative at its face value. When a bodily need produces a feeling of hunger, it seems to be I that am hungry, and not my body. If I adhere strictly to what I know, I cannot say that my body has a desire to be fed nor that it takes satisfaction in the eating: the discomfort and the pleasure are all mine. If I am told that in serving myself I am also serving my body; and that the whole situation may be read as the body's making use of the mind for the body's ends, I have two remarks to make. First, that I am pleased with this happy conjunction of interests so long as it lasts: but if the occasion comes when I have objects inconsistent with this service, I may impose upon myself a fast or a hunger-strike, and my body and I must then face together the consequences of my decision: the interest of the body can in no sense substitute itself for my own choice as the primary factor in action. My second remark is that strictly speaking my body has no interests and no ends to gain, no preference whether it be hungry or full, alive or dead. It is only as reflected in me that the body can be said to have desire; and though the body as seen by the biologist has a self-preserving character, this tendency can be read as a literal pursuit of an object only by dint of what Dr. Joseph Needham calls a "splash made by the entry of mental existences into the sea of inert matter"!* There is the further consideration that there can be no effective technical control of these mental decisions except *via* the mind.

We declined to build large hopes for

* *Science, Religion and Reality,* p. 251.

the mental future of the race on the "chemistry of the soul," except in so far as this chemistry affords a better control of normal health. But there seems reason to hope for a better physical future of the race by the aid of a sound mental hygiene. After the era of the charlatans has gone by, and to some extent by their aid, there appears a possibility of steadily enlarging self-mastery, as the spiritual sense of such discipline as the Yoga joins with the sober elements of Western psychology and a sane system of ethics. No one of these is worth much without the others.

But whether the apparent mental initiative is genuine, or merely technical, we can only decide by a more careful study of these causal cycles.

5. DUALISM RECONSIDERED

IT is time to reconsider our provisional dualism. I propose that we allow our imaginations to play for a moment with this curious fact of circular causation.

If we trace one of these cycles from the point where we first find it, namely, from the mind, it appears that the mind is caus-

ing certain changes in itself by way of the
body. Why must it go about these changes
so indirectly? Why must my thirst go out
of my mind in order to cure itself? Why
must my ill-temper produce changes in my
organic chemistry, stop my digestion, and
leave me depressed in order to bring me to
my senses? You say, because the causal
principle is involved. Thirst is a phenomenon with conditions; relief of thirst is another phenomenon with conditions: I must
comply with the conditions to pass from
the experience I dislike to the experience
I like. True: but does this paying of costs
take the causal series out of the mind?

Certainly it involves the body. But *unless the body is out of mind,* this fact does
not carry the causal series out of mind. I
am certainly aware of a series of stages in
the curing of my thirst. To be sure, I am
not explicitly aware of a million sub-micro-
phenomena which the physiologist might
mention; but I experience the salient causal passages in the event. And I experience also the connection between the disturbed equilibrium of wrath and the sub-
sequent deflation and chagrin as at once

causal and appropriate. It does not occur to me that the essential links of such bits of history are really out of mind.

Let me recall that I never experience any passage of events out of the mind into the body; nor is there any loss of the thread, as of a stream seeping into the sand. The sequence of events as I experience it is intelligible, though the physiologist supplies me with interesting details which escape my notice. Likewise, though events are all the time coming into the mind, I never discover them coming in *from the body,* as from an outer source. Thirst, for instance, I find not *from* the body but *in* the body as I perceive the body. And so with all other sensations. They come into the mind, it is true, unproduced by me: but not *from* the physical world, for they are the very raw material of the physical world.

If when I satisfy my thirst the causal series goes out of my mind into my body, I must have some view about my share in the performance. I lift the cup to my lips. What does this? My mind or my body? The physiologist will claim the muscular

response to thirst as in his province. The
dualist who tries to save a province for
the effective causality of consciousness, is
obliged to exercise his ingenuity to find
some residuum of the act which is not ex-
plicable in physiological terms. But the
mind *knows nothing about residues*. The
fact which consciousness knows is that "I
lift the cup and drink": what my body
does, I do. There is no talk here of dividing
efficacy between mind and body. The whole
act is mine. And as the body takes part in
it, the body must be somehow in me.

Is not the body a part of self? Does it
not consist of certain fairly constant elements of self-consciousness which, because
they are constant, I give no great attention
to, but which I should sorely miss if they
were absent? Let us name some of the more
conspicuous of these.

THERE is, first, this steady feeling of
homely warmth, as of the hearth-place of
life, a sense of *being,* which is usually a
sense of well-being. It is only by second
thought that I qualify this pervasive sense
of being as "bodily" warmth or as coenes-

thesia, and when I do so, I suspect that I have left something important out of it.

Then, there is a sense of *I-can, i.e.,* of manifold capacities which I cannot separate from myself—capacities to move, lift, write, see—each one with its definite amount and limitation. The limitation is as much a part of my sense of self as the power. I open the gate with so much exertion: I walk with ease at such a rate, and not much faster. These are my coefficients. And again, it is only by some afterthought that they are referred specifically to my body: the power of my limbs is my power —and in fact I never learn the physiology of my muscles: as I use it, I seem to live in it. These coefficients are fairly constant: I can do to-day approximately what I did yesterday with the same exertion. Any abrupt alteration of my powers, like an abrupt change of my appearance, would lead to a quizzical conflict of self-consciousness, and a disposition to enquire of outsiders whether "I be I, as I think I be."

Among these powers is the important power of contact with objects in the neighborhood of hands, trunk, feet, which I learn to attribute to my body as a visible organism in space.

Beside these I-cans are the *I-wants,* some of which, recurring and unbidden, I learn to localize in my body. The body which I serve, when I do serve it, is not the biologist's body, but the body-desire as I find it in myself; and a body-desire is simply a desire which I learn can be satisfied by some ministration to this spatial organism.

My body, then, enters into my experience as a visible object to which I refer certain wants and powers and my steady sense of being, now and here.

Is it not more natural, and more in accord with experience, to suppose that these circular effects we speak of, instead of wandering for a time in an alien order, and then returning, are working out their history *within the mind itself?* That hypothesis would be powerfully reinforced if, beginning with the mind, we could show that the body, instead of being an additional fact, is required by the mind as a part of its own being.

6. THE BODY AS A MEMBER OF
THE SELF

WHY do we need a body as a part of our self?

In the first place, in order to be a self we require a *clear distinction between thought and deed*.

It belongs to our kind of selfhood to contemplate action for a time before we do it. Certain philosophers have thought that with God contemplation and action are identical. For us this would be a destructive advantage. It is a part of our nature to contemplate many foolish and criminal deeds; it is a part of our moral being to do this. But it is also a part of our moral being that the contemplation of a crime is not a crime.

According to the Sermon on the Mount it is dangerous to be angry with one's brother; the murderous or lustful thought partakes of the quality of the action. But still, it is not the action. And what I want to make clear is that so long as the action does not take place, it cannot be said, even by ourselves, that we *really want to do it*.

The reason why dallying with an impulse
is so likely to involve mental conflict is
that we know, even while we dally, that
we are going to repress it before we are
through with it: there is already a division
in us at the threshold of consent. There is
a momentous difference between "my impulse" and "an impulse in me"; and often
it is not until I have finally acted upon a
wish that I am sure what "my wish" has
been. Even then, it stands waiting my sub-
sequent confirmation.

One reason why the continued contemplation of crime (as of murder or suicide)
is dangerous is that one acquires an artificial curiosity to pass that eternally tanta-
lizing barrier between the merely imagined
and the actual being. The rôle we feel is
a possible one: there is not a conceivable
failure or disreputable character but that
it might be I. How would it feel to be the
real thing? It is a hardship to be confined
to but one of the Protean possibilities of
our nature: and there is a clear relief in
throwing away repute and becoming once
for all the worst possible. If there is a hell
I shall not be satisfied until I go through

it and as Vergil rather than as Dante. But it is evident that this interest is something quite different from the original impulse to the violent deed; and that a thousand daily transitions from thought to action exemplify the same cosmic mystery.

This mystery is that it requires a deed to complete a thought. In a way, the preliminary thought is more perfect than any deed can possibly be: when I try to execute what I have contemplated, I somehow fall short or spoil it. Yet the deed is what I mean; and anyone who means good will without doing good will, or who means opposition without fighting, is suspected of the disease of sentimentality, which consists in living in the too pretty world of inoperative meanings.

Now the body, as we are directly aware of it, is this region in which thought first turns into actuality. Emotion is simply *thought becoming concrete,* showing its meaning in the body, and preparing for deeds of the body on outside objects. *Will* is the continuous consent to this embodying process, saying to a thought, "Be thou actual." At every moment of our lives, we preside over this mysterious transition without in the least understanding it. What the mind contemplates in purpose is always future; but the will as distinct from purpose is always present. Purpose enters into time; but will enters timelessly *into space*. A self without a body would be a self without a will.* The body, then, as a necessary condition for the possibility of will, is an essential region of the self.

We have to consider also that behind the will to do there is the *will to be,* which is far more constant. The will to be does not present the same bifurcation between contemplation and decision; we are hardly aware of a decision to be, for the will to be and being fall together. But the will to be, or "will to live," is also, in this sense, a decision, that it requires a consent not merely to exist in general, but to exist here and now, in this particular form and with these coefficients. I am not ready to say that to exist and to have a body are the same thing—though I think that to exist

* Note I do not say a self without this particular body would be without a will: hence I am not identifying the career of a self with the career of any given body.

and to consent to existence are the same thing; but I do say that to exist and to have particular existence are inseparable, and the body is to us that sphere of existence which is *completely particularized*. Immediate existence, for us, is existence as a being having sensation. Sensation is that sphere in which thought rests when it wishes to escape mere generality. In this sense there can be no mind without *matter* as a part of it: there can be no mind without a body.

IN the second place, in order to be a self, I require that my deeds shall leave an *accumulation of power* behind them.

The life of a self is a spreading circle of experiment—experimenting with new goods, and with new ways of reaching old ones. But if this moving on were like the progress of a grass fire, which has to leave its old ground or die, because there is nothing more there for it to live on the self would bear no resemblance to ourselves. As we move on, something is kept permanently. What I have done, I have gained a power of doing again. This requires mem-

ory, but also something more than memory. If a deed has brought a pleasing result, I not only remember doing it, but I
"know how" to do it, *i.e.,* I know that I can
do it again and with greater ease. I have
added something to a cumulative stock of
power, in the form of *active habit* or skill.

This accumulation is not something I
must separately try for; I rely on the
ability preserving itself, while I turn to
other things. No human infant seems to
worry, as its attention flits from one
achievement to another, for fear it should
be unable to recover the trick that pleased
it. I wonder at the admirable care-freeness
of the infant: it is as if it assumed from
the outset, not that it would be remarkable if it retained its achievements, but that
it would be remarkable if it did not! Modern science began when Galileo and Newton saw that a reason must be given, not
for the continuance of motion, but for its
cessation or change. With regard to the
persistence of acquired powers, the infant
begins with the spontaneous assumption
of something like Newton's first law—a
mind once competent remains competent

forever unless acted on by an external
agency!

This assumption is so much a part of
the very nature of selfhood that I despair
of exciting by these lame words of mine
any impression of its extraordinary character. It is clear, at least, that unless we
could turn away from any action to any
other whatever with complete confidence
that the cue to this prior action was in
some way being preserved without our effort, the self would be a much more ham-
pered, mechanical, and self-nagging affair
than the self as we know it. For this sense
of I-can, of which we were speaking, is
but the composite of all such acquisitions:
to be myself is to "know-how" to do a
thousand things named and unnamed, to
turn my eyes, walk, speak English prose,
read, cipher, drive nails, swim, open a co-
coanut, . . . And with the slow change in
these accomplishments, for indeed they do
not preserve themselves perfectly or forever, there is a corresponding change in
myself. But in so far as they do preserve
themselves, I know nothing about how it

is done. Or, more accurately, I am not
aware of doing anything about it.

The physiologist has no trouble in fur-
nishing hypotheses as to how it is done.
The "body" does it. There are hypothetical
brain-paths, trails blazed, the resistance of
synapses lowered, some sort of physical
modification which implies immense plasticity and immense retentiveness of change.
I judge that Professor Dunlap thinks that
this physical retentiveness is all we need.
"Memory," he says—and for the purposes
of the present argument, this would apply
equally to knowing-how—"does not imply
the laying of an 'idea' away in cold stor-
age for a time, and then later bringing it
out of the refrigerator. It merely means
that there is an abstract possibility of
thinking in a certain way, and that that
capacity depends on previous thinking.
But in the interval between thinking the
'thoughts' simply don't exist. . . . You
learn to make a shot by shooting: but in
the intervals between shootings there isn't
any 'shot.' "* What persists is the body
and its alterations.

* Knight Dunlap, *Old and New Viewpoints in Psychology*, p. 74.

I agree that this *principle of persistence* is included in what we mean by body, and that in this sense the mind needs a body in order to be itself. A habit or a skill may be called an artificial law of nature. It is a law of nature that fire will make water boil and that it will make a cold man warm: it always produces these effects in the same way. But if cold "stimulates" a man to build a fire, the Indian, the Russian, and the Zulu will each use a different method: his fire-building will follow the art he has acquired. His accomplishment is an artificial law of nature. In turning the habit over to nature, the mind is set free to be mind; and so routine is made to serve the interests of novelty.

But the habit or skill is *not all out of mind*. We never wholly banish from consciousness the deed that has been a source of satisfaction: a certain auspicious ghost of itself mingles with our new activities. What we dismiss is the physical detail of the performance. The absent deed remains with us somewhat as an absent friend, his manifold characteristics not distinguished, his quality concentrated, as it were, into a

single point which takes up no room in the
mind. To achieve a habit is to achieve simplicity in the thought of a deed; to know
how to swim is to lose separate concern
for the working of each arm and leg, and
to *swim!* Now this simplicity does not char-
acterize the physical performance: it is
found only in what the performance
means. We can keep our habits in mind,
without their occupying any room there,
because each one of them has a kind of
selfhood of its own, a meaning and a body.

The habit's self, *i.e.,* what the habit *is,* is
its motive or meaning and not its body.
This, as we saw, is a source of difficulty
for the behaviorist. The man who gives
money to this and that cause may be building up a habit of liberality: but if his motive is political influence or fear of the un-
popularity of refusal, the *self* of that habit
is not liberality, nor giving, but a polite
bribery or conformity. A habit is thus an
artificial natural law which never loses connection with its motive, and it swings in the
mind from the pivot of this motive, the
"self" of the habit.

It is because of this motive-kernel of

habit that it is always something more than a mere ability to perform; it is to some extent a desire to perform. This constitutes another difference between a man and a gun which the mechanist may overlook. The gun in the corner acquires no habit of idleness; on the other hand, it has no desire to shoot. But if the man can shoot, he is likely to experience the desire to shoot. For each habit, like a subordinate selfhood, has its own impulse of reincarnation. By building habits, the self becomes a colony of included and latent selves; and at each new experience the entire pack in leash is asking "What chance is there here for me?" A pond of water—and my boating or camping or painting habits prick up their ears. A new acquaintance—and my habit of impulsive onslaught or of protective retirement becomes alert. Once in conversation, whose essence is a mutual exploration into new paths, and certain threads of discussion, or certain stories, one's familiar "lines," are lurking for their opportunity to get into the open and win their old effect. These sub-selves have their wills-to-live.

Of course, they live only by my consent. Though the life of habit seems to beat with an independent will on the doors of the present, it is still I who am acting upon myself—not my body, nor even my past self, as something other. This momentum is something I wish to exist: it is a part of my own readiness and power. Personality may fairly be regarded—as by Watson and Dewey—as a sum of habits; but only because each habit is a product of personality, and its usable property. A child who "works up" in a swing gains a total momentum it cannot at once arrest, though the energy which resists stoppage is none but its own. A habit by its very success may similarly get into the way of a better sort of deed; but in this case, it is not necessary to "let the old cat die." For the *self* of an old habit is at once destroyed by the clear perception of its defectiveness. And with the loss of its life-principle, the physical body of the habit loses its aggressive force. "Conversion" as an abrupt alteration of habit is not only possible but relatively frequent both within and outside of religious experience. In the presence of a new enthusiasm, a new affection, or a new idea, old habits drop off like dead leaves.

Those who suppose that habit is a purely physical principle, and that the dismissed deed (or thought) simply ceases to exist as a conscious fact, thus lose sight of the most vital elements of habit—what the self of the habit is, its self-assertion and control, its displacement and death. Habit has its *body;* but that body is not out of mind! When I feel that I am "in command of myself," that means something more than that my body has certain abstract possibilities of action: it means a positive element of awareness that these possibilities are available. Were this not the case, our sense of self would be very different from what it is. For these possibilities in their sum constitute what we feel each moment as a *volume of selfhood,* a quantity with which, as an equipment, we are meeting experience.

The law of persistence, the law of momentum, and the law of volume, are doubtless laws of bodily facts; but they are at the same time laws of mental facts. This part of "nature" is an inalienable ingredient of the self.

THERE is another reason why the mind
needs a body—and this may seem the most
evident of all—namely, as an instrument
of *give and take* with the world beyond.
For the self is a system of purposive behavior; and behavior is nothing without a
known and definite world in which to be-
have. The self must be forever receiving
from this world, reacting to it, and making
it over. In order to carry on this intercourse, it must appear in the world in a
form akin to that world in structure, capable of being affected by its changes and
capable of effecting changes. This outer
world furnishes, as it were, the themes for
the activity of the self: it rains upon me
and I build my shelters; it makes me cold,
and I build my fires. And for the income
and for the outgo I must be *of* that world.
If it is bodily, I must be bodily. I cannot
chop wood by a purely spiritual will. The
self must be inserted in nature by way of
its body.

This argument is an appealing one, and
also a logically dangerous one. For it assumes that like can only interact with like.
And if this is true then all parts of an in-

teracting system must be physical or else all parts must be mental. We either give the body back to nature and leave the self out of the effective causal circuit; or else we bring nature with the body into the circuits of the self. Whether we can take this latter bold step may well give us pause; and we shall defer this problem for a later discussion. Meantime, at least this is true, that whatever nature is, the self needs its *place* there, identifiable and exclusive, its membership in the order of natural law, its continuous change of space-perspective, its force against force, weight against weight, its partnership in the struggles which constitute the economic and moral effort of the race. To be with its fellows in nature, it must appear bodily in nature.

We conclude that the self cannot be itself without its body. We must regard the body not as an appendage of the mind nor as a detachable instrument, but as an inseparable organ. The self is a system of meanings, but not of meanings without facts. The self is a hold on possibility, but not without its own actuality: it is an ac-

tual holding of possibility. The self has a
certain free-play among spaces and times,
but by way of will it becomes engaged in
this space-time order as an event among
events. The self is purposive, but to be purposive it must work as a cause among
causes. All the categories of the body are
required in the structure of the self.*

All this points in the direction of some
sort of spiritual monism. If mind had less
need of matter, we could more readily believe that matter could dispense with mind.
If mind requires matter for its own life,
the presumption becomes strong that body
and matter are somehow derived from its
life, and are at bottom of the same stuff
that selves are made of. We do not now
insist on this conclusion, but content ourselves with pointing out one consequence
of this intimate union.

Regarded as part of self, the body re-

* To Rignano, affectivity and memory are the biological groundwork of intellect. These categories correspond
closely to the categories of will and retention which are
in our view the mental groundwork of the mind's biological existence. The analyses agree; as for the interpretations, the latter would appear to me to absorb the
former.

sumes the rights which the sounder sense
of mankind has always given it. The meaning which descends from the central hope
of the self envelops the body: it becomes a
city of meanings, and not merely a city of
cells. Its organs are no mere facts, but
symbols, perilous and profound. It becomes as a whole an object of value, of
beauty or deformity, of grace and mechanism, of an implicit philosophy; and attitudes of pride and shame, the infinite interest of art, the versatile significance of
the dance, all become intelligible. Posture,
gesture, and a million subtle expressive
changes of color and tension become the
immediate indeliberate manifestations of
an inner play. Poetry and morality, religion and logic, regain their seat in our
members as well as in our minds, and the
world recovers the concrete unity of which
our analyses threatened to despoil us.

III.

THE SELF AND NATURE

7. A SERVANT OF TWO MASTERS

IF I say all I mean by "self," I cannot leave out the body. A self without a body, so far from being the freer and perfecter thing imagined by Plato, the Vedanta, the Sankhya, would be no self at all—at best a germinal, nascent promise of a self.

Body and mind are different: we have no intention of denying this proposition. But how are they different? Not as two distinct entities which somehow interact. Nor as two parallel sets of phenomena, each complete in itself. They are different rather as a part is different from the whole. The body is an organ of the self as the brain is an organ of the body. The self needs its body in order to be an actual, active, social, historical self.

In its day, Schopenhauer's philosophy was remarkable for the careful thought he gave to the position of the body in the scheme of things. For him, as for us, the body is certainly not something extraneous to the self. The body, he said, is the will—as seen from the outside: it is the will made visible or "objectified." The several organs of the body in different species and individuals reveal the peculiar traits of their wills.* The tiger's teeth and claws manifest his will to live by predation. The owl's eyes express a will to live by night-flying. The human brain and upright posture exhibit a will to live by thought and circumspection. There is a Lamarckian streak in Schopenhauer's philosophy of body: function is first and structure afterward. The goat and the bull do not butt because they have horns; they have horns because they butt. Every line of the body is what it is because the will is what it is.

No one before Schopenhauer had so fully done justice to the significance of bodily detail in revealing the traits of the volitional self. At the same time, for Schopenhauer the body was not a reality nor even a part of reality: it was a mere

---

* The several organs "correspond to the principal desires through which the will manifests itself: they must be the visible manifestation of these desires. Teeth, throat, and bowels are objectified hunger; the organs of generation are objectified sexual desire; the groping hand, the hurrying feet correspond to the more indirect desires of the will which they express." *World as Will and Idea,* tr. I, p. 141.

appearance of the self. There could be, for
him, no talk of the body as a part or an
organ of the self, sharing in the reality of
the self. He thought of it in one sense as
more than a part, since it revealed the
whole self to the outer eye. In another
sense it was less than a part, since it was
only a spatial symbol and not a real entity.

It is evident that Schopenhauer was not
thinking of the body as we are immediately conscious of it, but rather of the body
we see in others and use as a complete symbol for them. Inasmuch as whatever is visible is necessarily spatial, and empty of
sensitivity as well as of volition, there was
some ground for making this complete
separation between the inner view as pure
will and the outer view as pure body. But
if we consider the body primarily as the
body we are directly aware of, engaged in
all sensation and action, we cannot effect
this separation. The pure will is not fully
itself without *that* body. Volition for us *is*
a process of "objectification," an embodi-
ment. And the body becomes a symbol of
the self, a faithful and detailed symbol, because all the impulses of the self must real-

ize themselves by its agency. It is, or becomes, a perfectly fit organ of the self.

BUT have we not proved too much, or have
we not taken our hypothesis too quickly?
If the self cannot exist without the body,
are they not tied in an ominous union which
makes them partners in life and death?
And have we forgotten, in claiming the
body for the self that it certainly belongs
to nature? Can it completely serve two
masters? And is not the claim of nature the
prior claim?

Much as the self needs its body, it is not
at all clear that it makes it. "Objectification" is a brave word; but it is a metaphysical mystery. Our bodies appear to be
given to us; we have to learn them—a
great preoccupation of our early months.
It does not seem to me that I *know how*
to make my body. Samuel Butler, indeed,
holds that we, or something in us, has that
knowledge; for, he argues, what better
evidence can we have that we know how to
produce arms and legs, teeth and hair, than
the fact that we do produce them! But is
it we that do it? If we know how, that

knowledge is singularly unavailable in time of need!

Again, the body is certainly not altogether such as I will. Who is there that does not quarrel with his physical equipment? In what sense is Cyrano de Bergerac's nose an expression of *his* will to live? No doubt he required something to breathe through, but if the moulding of that organ is the work of an alien power our monism is destroyed: one's body is only in part one's own. Plato's strictures upon the body as a tool of the spirit have not wholly lost their force. To every I-can there is a limit: I can so much, but I can no more, whether for physical exertion or for thought, and this limit appears to have its seat and registration in the body, as if the body were the province of an alien power. It is not mind but body which interrupts my occupation with its demand for exercise or food or sleep.

There is an opposition here which Lord Dunsany has well put from the point of view of the delinquent member, "The unhappy body." The body complains, "I am united with a fierce and violent soul that

is altogether tyrannous and will not let me
rest, and he drags me away from the
dances of my kin to make me toil at his
detestable work!"* Such a soul may drive
matters to the point of divorce:

"I am tired of you. I am off," said the soul. And
he arose and went we know not whither.

"Now I can rest," said the body.

If the body is simply an element in the
self, how can such incompatibilities of temper exist? It is, in fact, more like a frontier
between self and not-self, and a function
of both. Like most between-things, it has a
wavering allegiance; and while in many
moods it appears to belong to me, in others
it becomes the agent and spokesman of the
outside powers. When appetite becomes
keen, as the appetite of Esau, it seems to
take possession and work its own will without much reference to the protesting self.
The passion of fear may take control of the
body and its deeds even against all habit.
And if fear is mastered by force of
thought, it is at the cost of distinguishing
once more between self and body. It is told

* *A Dreamer's Tales.*

of Turenne that at the beginning of a hot
engagement he found himself a prey of
violent trembling, while surrounded by
members of his staff. Instead of attempt-
ing to repress the humiliating ague he
turned on his body with the words, "Tremble body: you would tremble yet more if
you knew into what I am going to take
you!"

THE individual will to live has not all its
own way in making and managing the
body—certainly not so far as it is conscious. In order to represent the body as
the direct outer expression of the will,
Schopenhauer was obliged to enlarge the
conception of self to its subconscious
depths: and the body then becomes the
revelation or confession of much in the self
of which it is not aware. In Schopenhauer's
view, the body could never rebel in the
name of an outer power, but only in the
name of a hidden and contrary impulse of
selfhood.

Schopenhauer is right in pointing out
these deeper reaches of the self; and I believe, too, that he is right in supposing

that they are echoed in some of the apparent limitations of the body. But is he right, and are we right, in *beginning with the self?* Does the will produce itself? Is not every specification of the will which we see mirrored in the body the work of outside and prior forces? The traits of bird, tiger, man, have been beaten out in conflict with the world and are handed down in the species. How, then, can the bird's will to fly be called its own? It is a transmitted impulse, the impulse of the species.

It is true that the self is to some extent its own builder: it builds itself by way of habit; it becomes its own cause at the threshold of consent. But this appears a detail, an embroidery upon the mass of inherited selfhood. The will does not create and does not know its own sources. What are these sources? Whatever they are, they reside for a time, it seems, in two germ cells: they work by way of the body. The body, then, is first the agent of the other powers: it is the port of entry of new experience, and the channel of transmission of the hereditary determinants of will. The facts we must take account of are the facts

of this radical exchange between the self
and what lies beyond it, in birth, sensation,
death.

At birth, the self is provided with an
array of instincts, the elements of its heredity. In spite of all the mythology that
has been produced in the name of instinct,
and in spite of all the attempts to escape
the mythology by abolishing the name, instinct is an inescapable fact because heredity is an inescapable fact. Mr. John
Watson regards instinct as a "religious"
concept, because it has been used in an un-
scientific manner as a refuge for our ig-
norance. But there is no scientific advantage in substituting for the word "instinct"
the words "unlearned response"; and in
assuring us that there are almost no instincts or that we are "almost at the point
of throwing away the word 'instinct,' " but
that there are "thousands" of unlearned
responses! "An" instinct is, indeed, a more
or less arbitrary demarcation in the body
of our hereditary capital; but this hereditary deposit is the fact that counts. There
are dispositions in us which we can trace
to a general inheritance from the race.

There are others which belong to special
ancestral strains. Any self may be obliged
to recognize that some part of its fight in
the world is a direct bequest from a dis-
sipated forbear. And anyone may well believe that his capacity for pleasure is the
use of a capital energy built by the saving
and restraint of millions of ancestral or-
ganisms obedient to their vital impulse.

The body, then, is a portal, not a possession. And through this portal the self
peers out into a dark and cavernous back-
ground in which the perspectives of its
living past merge insensibly with the vast
shapes of physical nature.

8. THE STRANGER IN THE HOUSE

WE must consider the mystery of birth,
the reception of a transmitted selfhood.
But this is a place for resolution in holding to what we know. We have to recall that no one, from inside or outside,
ever observes selfhood being transmitted
through the world of physical nature. We
never observe any one of our impulses
arising *from* the body, as from something
beyond self, though they often arise *in* the

known body. For the most part, our current impulses seem to grow within the field of consciousness, or to shoulder their way from the margin to the center. And so it has always been with us from the beginning.

As some would express the matter, these impulses, particularly the profounder, instinctive impulses, appear as emerging from the "subconscious." For the most part our impulses are ways of dealing with specific types of occasion, and if the occasion is not present there is no impulse so to deal: it is only as a set of sensations which I learn to call hunger stealthily grow from nothing to something that the impulse to seek food emerges. Perhaps it is the sensation and not the impulse which comes from margin to center. But no; there are thinkers who attribute to impulse a more permanent existence, and who think of the major streams of impulse as racial, aboriginal, primitive, coming into the self from prior selfhood and living in the subconscious realm. The Freudian psychology is of this type.

THE "subconscious" as an obscure region, a mid-term between mind and matter, is under scientific suspicion. Professor
Knight Dunlap says that to refer a thing
to the subconscious is to refer it to an unknown and uncontrollable source; hence,
to do so is "religion" and not science. And
since according to Mr. Watson, it is religious to refer anything to instinct, the
Freudian psychology which uses both instinct and the subconscious must be doubly
religious! In spite of this grave charge, it
remains true that Freud and his followers
have lavished much shrewd observation
upon the original sources of mental states,
and I think not without valuable results.

For this school of psychology, the subconscious is the home in particular of that
fundamental instinctive trend which like
a turbid stream of racial impulse flows
through our being, always demanding out-
let and always unsatisfied and restless.
This craving, or "libido," or will-to-power
—it is perhaps best left nameless—is described in terms which suggest a disem-
bodied spirit or a dark, unruly stranger
whom we harbor as a secret guest while we

live our overt life in a critical, suspicious, and refractory world.

The analogy of the harbored stranger is not untrue to the Freudian theory; for this primitive, brooding impulse has aims as of a self distinguishable from my conscious self, whose aims are "rationalized" for the public gaze. Always uncertain of perfect welcome in this outer world, the fundamental urge dwells much in inner communion and dream. And in proportion as the given front of experience threatens more profoundly to thwart its wish, it reverts to earlier openings of the sky, juvenile outlooks, infantile, pre-natal perhaps; and rather than moving forward regresses toward paths even less congruent with the demands of outer reality. Thus, for example, religion arises as an imaginative cloaking of fact by fancies drawn from childish hopes of a perfect parental care, a symptom of defect of courage, or perhaps of the essential tragedy of existence which none are strong enough to face in its bald truth.

WE are not concerned with the Freudian

mythology; for its *dramatis personae,* with all pretence of scientific exactitude, are imaginative figures drawn by men groping as explorers must in a psychological twilight; they need not be supposed to fit the outline of reality more closely than the names of ill-discerned constellations in the skies. But we are concerned with the truth of that great trunk-stream of tendency which seeks, as an independent being, its life in the world; which has its ancient origins and its biological rhythms; and which maintains a persistent pressure against the inadequacies of our conventional social life. There is accuracy in the observation that this impulse has its epochs of impatience and danger, as at the turn of middle life, when it begins to sense the brevity of its hours of full flame and the uniqueness of this opportunity for self-expression. These years become dangerous, perhaps, just in proportion to the regularity and respectability of one's habits; because it is just these habits, confirmed by many memberships and friendships, which promise to perpetuate an anaesthetic routine centrally false to the profounder aspira-

tions of the man. They have lost their
moral value because they proceed by a momentum which belongs to the physical side
of habit. I say there is truth in this picture
for psychologists and sociologists; and for
social respectability as well.

But I suggest that we recognize the scientific inaccuracy of referring to this vital
urge as *other than the self*. To locate it in
the "subconscious" and speak about it in
the third person, as of a stranger in the
house, is a literary device which has its
scientific perils. It is *I* who am the stranger
in this world; it is *I* who am dissatisfied
with my own professions and my own
habits; it is *I* who lack the courage or the
skill to make my social self carry the full
measure of my will. This reversion now
and again to the outlook of childhood is
nothing else than the persistence of that
hope which, we have said, is the essence of
the self. The self which makes religion is
not a retreating self: it is the self which we
met at the outset, constructing its audacious picture of the universe, aware of its
destiny to deal with the ultimate powers.
Its religion is the sign of its courage, not

of its cowardice. My self is my hope; and my hope is forever unfulfilled, and forever reasserted. Call this hope by the more biological term, craving, or by the more romantic term, longing, *Sehnsucht,* or by the more metaphysical term, will—it is the same hope: it is *I,* and not an alien "it."

In William Watson's sonnet, *The Mock Self,* the rôles are with greater justice reversed: it is the overt self who is the alien, and the "subconscious" self, the central reality:

Few friends are mine, tho many wights there be
Who, meeting oft the phantasm that makes claim
To be myself, and hath my face and name,
And whose thin fraud I wink at privily,
Account this light impostor very me.
What boots it undeceive them, and proclaim
Myself myself, and whelm this cheat with shame?
I care not, so it leave my true self free,
Impose not on me also; but, alas,
I, too, at fault, bewildered, sometimes take
Him for myself, and far from my own sight,
Torpid, indifferent, doth mine own self pass;
And yet anon leaps suddenly awake
And spurns the gibbering mime into the night.

It is, of course, the prerogative of the self-conscious animal to think of himself

as of another, and to ascribe quasi-self-
hood to any of his impulses. This is clearly
in order with respect to those fragments of
heredity we call the several instincts. They
are sub-selves in the same sense as our
habits. They are the raw material of habit-
forming; and like habits remain attached
to the conscious self by the thread of their
meaning. They are all members of the
fundamental hope; and meaning, which is
single, descends from the whole to the
parts. These instincts may be "subconscious" in the same way that habit is subconscious when represented by a point of
meaning in the mind. But the great trunk
of impulse from which these instincts
branch out cannot be subconscious in the
same way. It is not a sub-self; for it is an
aspect of the whole self. It cannot be in
abeyance, for it is what I am: a craving
that is not felt is no craving at all, and a
craving that is felt by another than me is
simply not my craving. It is subconscious
only as the depth of consciousness is distinguished from its content; or as *that with
which* I am meeting experience is distinguished from the experience being met. To

every item of experience the self is saying
both Yes and No: Yes, it is good; No, it
is not yet that good I hope for. Which of
these judgments is more constant and emphatic, God knows. But the self, the longing, is the author of both of them, hence
never away from the focus of living,
though seldom occupying that focus as its
own sole object. The stranger in the house
is no other than the host himself.

Now all this means that when we seek
for the sources of the self in the "subconscious" we are seeking the sources of the
self within the self! The subconscious is no
mid-term between mind and matter, no obscure passageway from body to mind: the
subconscious is a region within the self.*
The self cannot discover its own temporal
beginnings by this route, nor by any other
mode of burrowing from within.

IF we think of the origins of a new individual solely from the facts which an out-

* A more detailed discussion of the subconscious may
be found in an appendix to my book, *The Meaning of God
in Human Experience*.

side observer can discover, it may easily
appear that while the new body is continuous with the parental bodies, the new mind
is quite distinct and discontinuous. It seems
that the body is first formed, and that the
mind then gradually supervenes; in which
case, the hereditary determinants of character must have had for a time some form
of sub-mental or latent existence. Each
new self is clearly a consequence of conscious deeds of prior selves: but it is commonly an unpremeditated and sometimes
an unwelcome consequence, and if the new
self cannot be said to be *meant* by its parents there can be no volitional continuity
between them and it—its will is not a
carrying on of their wills. For its part, it
can hardly be said to have contemplated or
intended those parents. If it could regard
its life as a gift, and as an unintentional
gift, might it not with equal detachment
pass judgment upon it and, conceivably,
decline it? Is the new will not a completely
new and independent fact in the world?

Assuredly these suggestions are ground-
less fictions: in dealing with mental origins, the external view can give us strictly

nothing but the biological facts. In inter-
preting them, we can at least avoid the
Freudian fallacy of distinguishing between the new self and "its" impulse. The
new self *is* its impulse: it is a new will to
live; *to be, for it, is to accept being*. It can
only exist as an incipient, groping will,
embodied in a few elementary dispositions
to action. For the use of these instincts or
unlearned responses it is in the strange position of having an initial technique, as if
they were *habits*—but habits it had not itself acquired; and also some sense of the
meaning of these actions, as if it had a
memory of the outcome—but a memory
not based on its own experience! Let us
be clear that an impulse can only exist as
having a time-direction: in its very first
moment, it must have a direction toward
the future, and this is inseparable from
a direction toward the past. The very conception of a beginning of conscious life
carries with it a paradoxical reference to
something prior to that beginning—as it
were a sort of Platonic reminiscence. It
thus lies in the nature of the case that as
we examine our own duration in time,

tracing our memory backward to the utmost, we can find no wall of partition between self and prior-to-self. I never know
by introspection how old I am, or that I
have a finite age. If the impulse which is I
is a "racial impulse," there is no reason to
ascribe age to it: it is presumably, like
energy, always new as on the first day.

It is, in fact, a gratuitous assumption
that where one self begins another must
stop. The truth is rather that different
selves overlap: the continuity of the body
is outdone in the continuities of the mind.
The selves have many objects in common;
presumably they have also some community of desire and tendency. If the body
of one may be, for a time, a part of the
body of another, may not their impulses
and memories be also shared? Here we
are, indeed, thrown back on speculation.
But at any rate, there is no evidence that
in reproduction the mental life passes
through a bodily sojourn: so far as heredity is concerned, we may still hold to
our view that the body is part of the self.

9. NATURE THE CONSUMER

EVEN so, we have merely postponed the major difficulty. Granted that these anterior forces which bequeath to us our bodies and therewith our instinct-capital are mental forces; and granted also that every new I-will is so far coincident with these earlier I-wills that it may fairly claim its inherited body as a part of itself. Granted that the wings of every new-hatched bird express its own will to fly and not merely a parental impulse to affirm and continue their own mode of life. Still, all such selves are immersed in the greater total, nature. Parents and offspring alike, as to their bodies, are parts of physical nature; how, then, can any self lay claim to its own body unless it is prepared somehow to lay claim to all of nature with it?

The solidarity between the body and nature is of the closest. Given the bone, Cuvier could reconstruct the fish: given the body, the ideal scientist could reconstruct the physical universe—the two are of a piece. They are of a piece, also, in respect to my will: as I need the body, so I need

nature. If my need of the body implies
that the body is a part of the self, does
not my need of nature, by the same logic,
imply that nature also is part of the self?
Our hypothesis seems to lead us back by
an indirect route to that subjective idealism or solipsism which we rejected at the
outset.* If that view is to be discarded,
must we not give up our hypothesis and
allow that physical nature is the all-con-
suming totality of which selves are but peculiar parts?

Now we clearly reject the subjective
view of nature: the self, as we said, is but
half of the world it perceives. Solipsism is
but half true! It has a half-truth which we
must acknowledge, namely, this: While the
self is receiving, not making, the world it
perceives, and is at every point in contact
with a not-self, it proceeds at once to create after the pattern of what it perceives.
Shut your eyes, and the visual world does
not cease for you: if the field of your vision
contained moving objects, their motion
continues before you†—you are actively

* Page 104, above.

† If you are following the uniform motion of a well-

reproducing and anticipating the course of your experience. To expect is to build in advance of the fact. The self has some power to produce from its own resources a world coextensive in quality and quantity with nature: and when we dream or daydream, we project from these inner resources an environment for the body together with the body. Imagination constructs body and world in a piece.

But imagination we regard as an imitator: its products, we say, are not "realities." In the real order of things, nature lies beyond the self, not within it: and nature claims the body. Our question, then, amounts to this. If nature is not-self, is it so foreign to us that we cannot claim *joint ownership* with its alien proprietor—if it has a proprietor—much as we claim joint interest in the transmitted impulses of heredity? An inventor receives a bequest which enables him to finish his experiments, to patent and market his invention: is the invention therefore *not his own?*

marked object, as of an aeroplane moving across the sky, you will find on opening your eyes after a brief interval that your gaze has moved with the object, and still catches it.

What is received is the material equipment
for bringing his idea to earth: the idea is
still his idea and no other's. Here we
readily admit that it is the idea which determines the ownership, not the raw material: it is the idea which organizes and gives
meaning to that material inheritance and
determines what it is. Is there some analogy between this case of received material
and that immense and continuous influx
of material-for-experience we call nature?

PERHAPS the description of nature as material-for-experience takes too much for
granted, since it labels nature by a rôle
which it plays in consciousness. The difficulty of our problem lies in the apparent
independence of nature: it is something for
us, but it is also something on its own account. What we have to do is to consider
those qualities which make nature appear
so durably self-sufficient and independent,
if not an alien realm.

Two of these qualities we shall pass over
briefly, not because they are unimportant
but because they are involved in others—
the limitless immensity of nature in space

and time, and the vividness or intensity of
natural fact, its inescapable thereness. The
mind, as we have seen, is unspatially related to the whole of space—and more!—
and untemporally related to the whole of
time—and more! The self is contained in
both space and time, but not *simply* contained: the relation is reciprocal. As for
the vividness of natural fact as compared
with imagination, impressive as it is, it is
evidently a matter of quantity rather than
of principle. Besides these there are three
marks of nature's otherness. First, the simple *given* quality of sense-data, colors,
sounds, smells, tastes; we have to discover
them in order to know them, we could
never have invented them, we cannot de-
duce them as necessary features of the universe from any known rational principle.
Second, the relentless order of nature, pursued with exact lawfulness without reference to my will or yours, and apparently
also without any will of its own. Third,
the publicity of nature: it always appears
as observable by others as well as by myself.

First, as to our sense-data, the original

stuff of our experience of nature. I do not
say the original stuff of nature; for what
the ultimate ingredients of nature are, science is not ready to say. Our experience
of nature begins with these sense-qualities,
sights, tastes, etc., in space and time; and
we cannot sufficiently wonder that it is
just these qualities which traditional
physics rejects as being in us and not in
the objective world. Under the name of
"sensation," psychology has commonly accepted the disowned qualities and made
them, if not the head of the corner, at least
the foundation of the mental edifice. But
let us not hasten to claim these properties
for the self; for certainly in our experience of nature these sense-data appear as
ingredients of nature. Let us give full
credit to that appearance, and respond
whole-heartedly to the summons of Professor Whitehead to avoid the "bifurcation of nature." Only, let us be clear that
when we mount colors and sounds in their
proper setting in space and time, and call
the whole concrete picture by the name of
nature, we thereby definitely reject a common illusion, namely, that sense-data are

caused by nature. This is the most pal-
pable of confusions. For how can that be
caused by nature which is the very fabric
of nature? If we regard nature as the cause
of our experience, we are bound, with Descartes and Locke, to "bifurcate," and re-
sign sense-data once for all to the self. If
we decline to bifurcate, nature is not the
cause of sensations.

If then we seek a source for sense-data
beyond themselves, as we must, it is *beyond nature* that we are obliged to go: and
nature has surrendered its apparent independence and self-sufficiency. And so far
as we are dependent upon sense-data for
our experience and our being, it is not nature upon which we depend: it is rather
that ulterior being upon which nature also
depends.

As a second mark of otherness, we note
that *strict lawfulness of nature's action,*
which bends to no man's will. For many
thinkers (especially those of the Kantian
schools) the element of law in events is the
chief element in their independence of us
and of our will—their standing over

against the mind as something other, their "objectivity."

Now when we say that nature is a realm of law, what we mean might be put by saying that nature is occupied in *drawing consequences*. You ask, consequences of what? The naturalist replies, Consequences of previous events, which are themselves consequences of still earlier events. Then nature is drawing consequences of consequences of consequences . . . ! This answer, though it has all the form of truth, and is quite verifiable, is evidently the absence of an answer or its indefinite postponement.

We should have a substantial answer only if we could find in the world something capable of *starting* a chain of consequences. Unless our analysis has deceived us, the will is precisely such a thing: for will, we thought (see page 81), in the moment of decision is effecting the transition from contemplation to actuality, from possibility to being. Will is a realizing or actualizing principle of the world, as we know it: and for the sake of the argument, let us hypothetically accord to it the initiative it appears to have.

Now the will is perpetually engaged in deeds whose consequences it only partially discerns. You undertake a journey with a friend; and every day of it brings unexpected situations and new tests of the quality of that friendship. It is largely for the sake of such discoveries that you undertake the adventure. No man knows all that he does when he does any deed. No geometer knows all that he does when he draws a circle. Least of all does anyone know what is implied in his will to live. These implications, however, are drawn for him. Who draws them? Nature. For nature is the sphere in which all the immediate implications of any fact are instantly drawn, and in which all the consequences of any fact are drawn in due time.

We do not know in advance what is implied in our own wills; but we proceed to find out. And it is *a part of our will that we shall find out*. We desire and will this inherent consistency of experience which relentlessly annexes to every deed its consequences, and thereby instructs us in the

wider reaches of our own meaning. To be
in this sense responsible and rational is a
part of the purpose of every purpose: it is
implied in the will to live.

This lawfulness of nature, then, which
seemed to set nature apart from the self,
begins to appear as something implied in
the nature of the self: and I can very well
fancy myself in the position of our inventor, to whom what comes from outside becomes with all its laws bone and blood of
his own idea. This would certainly be the
case if nature were engaged in drawing
only the consequences of my own will-acts.

But it is a part of nature's sublime im-
partiality that I receive at every moment
the consequences not only of what I have
done but also of what countless others, my
contemporaries and predecessors, known
and unknown, have done together with
much which apparently nobody has done,
and which has no intelligible relation to my
meaning. Some of these consequences are
surely alien to my will. If I can adopt them
as mine, it can be only by way of some ex-
tremely hospitable ingredient of my will
which I do not find on the surface. It would

have to be a trait of will which establishes some community of destiny between me and these other wills, whose consequences nature bears to me. I believe that there is such a trait, and that we shall discover it in the third mark of otherness.

WE have said that nature is other than self because it is *public*. It is a common object for many selves: they form an immense group in space and time with respect to this common object: if it is property for any of them, it is property for all of them, and hence private property for none of them. Each must respect it as also belonging to others.

There is much in our attitude toward nature to bear out this idea of common property. Nature is "real" as over against my private fancies, dreams, imaginations. It is real because it is the world of our common life. I have an obligation to the space and time of nature, because I have an obligation to you. Buried in my books, oblivious of my appointments, living in another space-time world, I am disloyal to my comrades. The shame of living in

drug-dreams or intoxication is not its
pleasure, and it would still be shameful
though there were no accompanying decay
of mentality: its shame is its subjectivity,
the abandonment of the common task in
the real world of common objects, the
abandonment of these my others.

The ideal accuracy of nature indicates
to what degree we are concerned in the
agreements of social life, the exact courses
of navigation, the location of meridians
and boundaries, the precise timing of
clocks. Here our wills, the wills of this vast
company, are in identical accord. Perhaps
no two immediate interests are in more direct opposition than those of pursuer and
pursued. Each would wish his own miles
to be shorter and those of his opponent
longer. Yet it occurs to neither to rebel
against the fundamental condition of their
actions, that each mile shall be precisely
the same for both.

The publicity of nature—if we may take
this as its primary sort of otherness—thus
throws some light on its lawfulness; for a
world which is to serve many wills at once
must be impartial as only an ideal law is

impartial. It also helps to explain the
inanimate, "dead," mechanical character
which we associate with this lawfulness in
the inorganic world. For whatever is ani-
mate or living we feel bound to treat with
regard, in proportion to its degree of life:
we cannot ruthlessly break and reshape
what is conscious nor grind it in our ma-
chines. If nature were sensitive in detail to
its last recesses, the work of the plow, the
spade, the axe, yes, even the simple movements of men would be attended with such
death-dealing and pain-giving as would
render effective living at last intolerable;
we should sink stages deeper into the predicament of the enlightened Buddhist; we
should be beset at every turn with such
questions as Mr. G. K. Chesterton pro-
pounds—"Why should salt suffer?"* The
inanimateness of nature confers freedom
to exploit and reshape: the circumstance
that it is a world of facts and not of mean-
ings† makes it the perfect receptacle for
such meanings as we will to impose upon
it. It can enter unobtrusively into works

* *Napoleon of Notting Hill.*
† Above, p. 35.

of public utility or beauty because its mechanical base is neutral and unconscious in its minutely lawful procedures. A world of conscious enterprise and especially of social enterprise would be impossible without such an impassive base: a world of meanings would necessarily include, and so give meaning to, such a world of the meaningless as abstract physical nature affords.

Thus while nature cannot be said to belong to any single self, it can be well understood as belonging to a community of selves: it is not within any one of them, but it might be an identical part of all of them. It would be over against each one of them, as an independent realm, because all the other selves are over against each one: their distinctive concerns would lend to it for each self an "objective" character. Nature would be independent and objective in a relative and derivative sense, not in an absolute sense—a conclusion which was suggested also by our study of sense-data.

Is it reasonable to consider nature as such a common domain belonging to many selves at once? This hypothesis would explain many of its striking characters, including those which set it in the sharpest contrast with the world of mind. But it would hardly be a reasonable hypothesis unless the many selves that live on this infinite world of nature can be said to have some identical element in all their wills. Can any such fundamental community of will be thought to exist? I believe that it does exist; and that it is the original relation of this enormous and loose-bound community of selves to each other. How this may be, let me now briefly try to suggest.

IT needs no argument to show that our human wills to live are always wills to live *with others*. The least social of men is inescapably sociable, not by overt choice, but by the nature of such finite minds as we are.* For us, to live is to grow; and the craving for growth itself grows by what it feeds on, and so seizes as its own that most potent and endlessly cumulative agency of growth, association with others,

* For a more elaborate analysis of sociability, see *Man and the State,* Part III.

reaching out through time and space. We need to be with other selves, not accidentally nor by convention and special effort, but by a kind of inescapable insertion and natural access, capable of all degrees of distance and all degrees of intimacy. We need that kind of with-ness which is best defined as simply being in the same world, for this kind of being together involves no oppressive closeness, and yet allows infinite possibility of approach and rapport. It is not difficult to find groups of selves which have so organized their conversation, their distances, and their meetings, that they aid one another's growth. The members of such a group have an identical ingredient of will, namely, the will to live with each other.

Any such group is obviously very limited in comparison with the innumerable company of selves which in all time have participated in this universe. In most of these one can claim no manner of personal interest; and some he may actively wish out of existence. But in spite of himself, his will extends to them by its logic. For something of all association adheres to the growing mind: to associate with any person is to associate vicariously with his associates. To put it barbarously, the relation of mental with-ness is transitive: if A is with B, in this sense, and B is with C, then A is with C; for B, having associated with C is now, whether he likes it or not, and always, *B with C*—that is what he *is!* Such a chain of intercourse clearly extends without limit to all participants in any historical nexus.

This only states in a highly mechanical and imperfect fashion what we are intimately aware of without analysis, namely, that our wills are not so many specimens of an abstract type: they are individual wills to live with specific other individuals in an order we call *historical,* in which every event and every idea is what it is because of what has gone before it and what accompanies it. To live here and now as *this* self is to live in context with *these* others, whether I know them or like them or not. In this will to live historically with these selves we have an ingredient of will which may be called identical in all members of this vast and dispersed company.

And thus to will is to require that common medium through which intercourse with them is possible, namely, nature.

I certainly do not know *a priori* that existence with these other persons implies the peculiar arrangements of my body, breathing, eating, etc. I could not have deduced my own head and trunk, arms, legs, eyes, nose: still less those complex internal arrangements which remain to me, and perhaps to all men for all time, a world of abundant wonder. No "deduction of the categories" by any philosopher has penetrated far into the necessity of these details.* Certainly, too, we discover in and

---

* It is perhaps not possible to show that a world, common to many minds, *must be a world of space;* but space as we know it is such a common world. Each self has a vested interest in the whole of this space: this space is therefore present indifferently to all of these communicating minds; and the contents of space, or nature, are a region in which minds come to coalescence. As a system of behavior, each self appears among the contents of this world as an object among objects, visible as a body to each other self. And since each body is responding to the whole of physical nature, it must contain within it a part which can be put into correspondence, point for point, with all the points it can distinguish in that world: that is, space must approach the structure of an infinite manifold; and further, that of a manifold whose finite parts are infinitely divisible. The brain, as a spatial mir-

out of the body many a fact we do not, in its separate capacity, want, many a fact which is evil, and so to be changed or destroyed. But so far as such facts are unchangeable, they are the actual cost of my will to live. De Bergerac's nose is not the nose of his choice. But it is the nose which, if he were to take his place in nature, and be *himself,* the offspring of these parents, with them and their "withs," he *had to have.* His nose is a consequence of an act of his own will, the acceptance of this life; it is a consequence drawn by nature, but still his; and it is in this quality that he feels a chivalrous regard for it, and proposes to defend it against all comers.

NATURE is other than me and before me. But there is nothing about nature which

ror of the intercourse of its self with its world, must be able to represent, as in a metaphorical analysis, each distinguishable phase of mental life. And thus the body becomes—roughly in its superficial aspect, and accurately in its less accessible aspect—a *set of signs* in which the observer can read the passing states of the self there acting. He cannot see those states; but he can see the translation of them into the spatial language. And of his own brain-events, he can say, This is not my self; but it is the translation of my self into the special set of hieroglyphics which we call physical.

I cannot adopt and use, as the inventor adopted his bequest, or Cyrano his nose. In all its types of otherness, factual, legal, social, it shows itself to be fitted for taking part in the life of self—not merely fitted to be known, nor fitted to be used in the arts, but fitted in its structure for interplay in the development of the will. Its very dead impersonality, the most alien of its traits, is essential to qualify it for serving as a non-intrusive common region in the will-life of many selves at once.

We may therefore accept to this extent the at-first staggering implication of our theory that the body is an organ of the self, namely, that nature is also such an organ. I cannot be myself without all of nature in space and time. The environment of any body is a part of the fact we mean by body. To the salmon after thousands of miles of sea-wandering there is just one stream in the world where it can breed and die: that stream is carried with it in the implications of its own body, and presumably also of its sense of being. It is not less true of higher creatures that their worlds of fact enter into the definitions of their selves.

But nature belongs to me only in so far as I make it mine: it does not cease to be also other-than-me. It remains, I suspect, other and prior to all of us, because it is first the work and organ of a profounder self. Our lives are spent in learning what nature may mean for us: our appropriation is still superficial. Only, we know that nothing in nature is ultimately alien. We receive first, but we reproduce afterward. As in heredity, the stranger became the host, so in natural causation the consumer becomes the consumed. The self is the organizing principle: it is thus the superior, the owning principle. In this circumstance lies its freedom.

IV.

FREEDOM

10. FREEDOM FROM WITHIN

IN ancient Arabia, Mamun, son of Harun al Rashid, inherited a city. When he came to take possession, he found it in disorder and on the verge of ruin. Persian traders, falling into dispute with the citizens in the markets, had found them weak and had become emboldened to pillage and violence.

The young prince was advised to set forth a new code of law and enforce it. This he did; but with the result that disputes multiplied, the lawyers enriched themselves, the citizens were impoverished, and traders began to avoid the city. In despair, Mamun bethought himself of a device. He secretly brought together certain foreign craftsmen, and enjoined them to work out in ivory and precious woods the image of a surpassingly beautiful city, whose design he gave them. When it was finished, he rewarded them richly and sent them away; and bore the image by night to the chief mosque, concealing it behind a curtain.

Mamun then issued an edict that every

traveler and trader entering the gates must
first be brought to this mosque to worship,
and be pledged to silence. The image was
there revealed to them; and it became evident to the citizens by the altered de-
meanor of these strangers that they had
seen a noble vision of which they could not
or dared not speak. They demanded to see
it also—which was what Mamun had de-
sired: they were accordingly admitted, one
by one, on the same conditions.

Now it began to appear that the ruler of
the artists was more successful than the
ruler of the law-makers; for, changed by
the sight of the image, the people carried
out their business in peace. Order, gaiety,
and wealth returned silently to the place.
And in its rebuilding, the city which Mamun inherited resembled the city of his
dream.

FOR our purposes, this city may represent
a self, the citizens its instincts and habits,
and the traders the lines of natural causation that run into it and out of it. Without
these citizens and traders, no city. Without
their laws, no city. But together, these ele-

ments are incapable of providing unity or common life. This life depends on the hope, or vision, which is the source from which meaning descends to the parts. And freedom is represented in the fact that, when that hope is active, the *detail of behavior is different* from what it would otherwise have been. It is behavior which belongs to that hope or meaning, and not primarily to the causal laws which it observes.

Since there is no self without its hope, there is no self which is not free. Freedom is not an attribute of the will; it is the essence of selfhood. As the meaning descends into all parts, freedom pervades the entire self of behavior. It is not that the mind, as purposive, is free, while the body, as causal, is determined; it is I as a whole that am free. What my body does, I do. All the determining influences that would pass to the control of my muscles must stop at the source of meaning and receive its stamp.

This meaning itself has no earthly source: it is the self as artist that has produced it. For the self is a new fact in the world; its perception of good is its own; and the hierarchy of control which it estab-

lishes has its apex in a unique perception
of possible value.

The prince in the allegory set up his
image and left it to do its work. But the
self is always destroying its old images and
making new ones, with an endless train of
foreign suggestions passing through its
workshop. The identity of its hope is not
destroyed in this process of growth. But
as the self expands, the material swept
into its organization of behavior becomes
greater; and a new chaos furnishes the
theme for a new construction. It belongs
to selfhood to increase without limit the
mastery of meaning; hence it belongs to
selfhood to grow without limit in material
depth and rootage. It requires an infinite
material universe to open the future to the
infinite appetite of freedom.

In the cycles of causation we were
studying, the appearance of initiative with
the mind proves to have been a true appearance. The threshold of consent marks
the entry of meaning into that circuit, and
the submission of the whole process to the
ownership of the self.

THOUGH every act of a living self is a free act, there are special occasions in which freedom is realized from within in contrast to a course of behavior relatively unfree. These occasions are the acts of *reflexion*. Reflexion is an experience in which the self turns and looks at itself, makes itself an object of contemplation, and becomes more or less aware of the difference between the self as observed and the self it desires to be.

When the self thus observes itself, it is to some extent *detached from what it sees*. A degree of independence is established between the self observing and the self observed; so that what the self judges the self to be is at once true and untrue. Let us say that in the order of nature I am a lazy man. Then I remain a lazy man, thoroughly subject to the causal laws of inheritance or habit, until such time as it may occur to me to observe my own laziness. But let me, in a moment of reflexion, recognize this trait, and judge "I am lazy." The judgment is true: yet it is not the whole truth. For I am also a man who observes and criticizes his laziness. This criticism is possible because of some standard, belonging to my hope—some standard of what a man might well be. In this moment of reflexion, or self-judgment, the self has in its power the beginning of a departure from laziness. Reflexion is a beginning of freedom.

The fact that the knowing mind, the subject, has or acquires a certain independence of what it observes, its object, has been recognized in various currents of thought, as by the realists of to-day. The realists are prone to insist that the object known is completely independent of the knower, even (one must suppose) when the object is one's self. We need not go to this extent: it is enough to see that when we judge ourselves we continue to make the usual distinction between the self judging and the object judged. This is particularly true when we "stop to consider" or contemplate our object as in a picture: for as mankind from Aristotle to Schopenhauer has repeatedly observed, the contemplator (whether as artist or enjoyer) is detached in will and being from what he considers.

The implications of this detachment are

far-reaching. When I perceive myself as
defective or limited in any respect, I am
in that act somewhat beyond this defect
and limitation: to be somewhat beyond it
is a condition of being able to observe it.
Then I am a shade beyond any limit that
I can discover: and there is, in this capacity of reflexion, a promise of indefinite
growth. Infinitude is on the side of the self
which knows itself to be finite. And for
the self which knows itself to be caused,
causation has ceased to be the whole truth.

Now there is nothing in the field of natural
causation entering into me upon which I
may not thus reflect. And to discover a
cause in the act of affecting me is to be
upon my guard against its action. Hence
any series of natural consequences which
flows up to me becomes distinct from me
when I discover it. If I find that my body
is the last term in some evolutionary series,
I cease to be that last term. *I am never
merely the last term of any series which I
observe.* The clock strikes twelve: to the
physical order, the last stroke is the last,
and no other. To me who listen it is

"twelve"; for I am keeping the others in mind with it. I am *with* the other strokes while I am with the last stroke: so that what is true of the last term of such a series is never all the truth about *me*.

So the description of a man as a set of reactions becomes untrue when he becomes aware that he is being so described. Whenever anyone knows what reaction a given stimulus is supposed to produce, he has a new motive for not acting that way. In certain writings on the psychology of advertising, I am told that the picture of a domestic scene will tend to soften the purchaser's heart and so to loosen his purse strings: when next I see this domestic scene in an advertising page, my heart hardens, and I inwardly refuse to buy.

Because of this trait of freeing himself by reflexion from every causal series he discovers, it is never possible to know all the reactions of any man. If any psychologist or friend thinks that he knows all the reactions of any individual, he has only to tell him so, and he will get a new one! Let anyone discover that he is behaving in any situation like a reaction-mechanism and he will feel toward that behavior perhaps an excess of repudiation, for very fear of resemblance to that which he most dreads, the inanimate machine.

Hence any program, which like that of the behavioristic psychology, aims through the scientific knowledge of human nature to "predict and control" our behavior, as agriculture hopes to predict and control the response of crops to different fertilizers and soils, can only succeed so long as it is kept a profound secret. You can only "manage" men through "stimuli" so long as they do not know that you are managing them! There is no more futile undertaking in the world than that of "applying" a cause-and-effect psychology. Books on applied psychology, on being published, begin the process of defeating their own aim. As a law of history becomes untrue by being known and stated, so does every alleged law of conscious behavior.

IN contrast with this spurious and self-defeating management of men by way of stimuli and causation, there is the honest management which follows the reverse procedure. Instead of trying to control the man by way of his physical situation, it controls the physical situation by way of the man's conscious choice. A naval officer writing of the management of men touches the right spring in the following bit of advice to fellow officers:

Suppose our first sailing launch under care of Bill Jones, coxswain, has continually fallen below the required standard of cleanliness. . . . By heckling and driving we may finally get the boat fixed up for inspection—and thereby have accomplished a little. But if we are able to get Bill Jones himself fixed up, to get him to take a pride and intelligent interest in his boat, then we have accomplished as much and a great deal more . . . Bill Jones has become an asset instead of a liability, and the seed thus sown tends to multiply itself.*

Captain Parker does not tell us how to get Bill Jones fixed up. If there were any infallible rule for doing it, the locus of freedom would transfer itself from Bill Jones to the manager of his choices. All that can be done is to present to our coxswain the vision of a clean sailing launch and its implications, in the reasonable hope

* Captain Parker, *Naval Institute Proceedings,* March, 1924.

that he may catch sight of the beauty of cleanliness, admit it to a place among those new stimuli which we are all so cautious about, and eventually fall in love with it because it legitimately belongs to his own sort of hope. This is the only way to "get Bill Jones."

In sum: the nature which is known as an object of thought can never reduce the self to a link in its own chains of causation.* *Reflexion* upon the self-in-nature situation automatically provides the self with *another alternative* than the uniquely determined causal outcome. With the one space-and-nature before it as object, it can conceive possible others, and choose among them. The self is free from the single-series determination of whatever it makes its object.

11. FREEDOM FROM WITHOUT

FREEDOM, from the internal point of view,

---

* This is quite independent of the question whether the self does or does not "give laws to nature," or whether the causal laws which the mind discovers in the world of physics are its own ways of putting that world into order. I am not asserting that the order of nature is in any sense subjective, or purposely posited, or illusory.

is found in reflexion or self-awareness.
What is freedom from the external point
of view? Can the scientific view of man as
a part of nature make any place for the
freedom thus internally described?

I think it must allow such a place. There
are two ways of disposing of freedom without altering the physical view of human
behavior; but I cannot adopt them. The
first is by holding that causal necessity is
merely an external reading of the sequences whose inner reality is purposive
and free. Kant seems to have held this
view; Schopenhauer also, and many others.
Causality, these thinkers agree, is without
exception or seam or fault: but since causality is merely the outer record of an inner striving, freedom remains the primary
truth. When I am asked to accept this
equation between freedom and mechanism,
I think of a lifted dagger: and I ask myself the question whether it shall or shall
not fall upon its victim. Is the issue of
that physical behavior already settled in
the previous conditions of the universe?
Then, however the agent may acknowledge the deed as his own wish, he was not

free to do otherwise. The sense of freedom is an illusion.

The second way is to hold that the issue is misstated: the causal principle in some way fails to apply to the mental flux. Thus, it is held that causality obtains only between separable events which are distinguished by intellectual analysis, whereas mental life has no such separable parts— there is nothing which can stand outside the act of will as cause to effect. This is Bergson's resort. But again I recall the lifted dagger; and I see that the only freedom I am concerned with is a freedom which makes differences in the physical plane, a freedom of alternative possibility *within the field of fact,* be it intellectually analyzable or not. This way evades the question.

IT is a literally indeterminate future for which we must provide, in our view of nature, if freedom is to have the sense we ascribe to it.

This is sometimes understood to mean that we must somehow find a mechanical explanation of the free act. Hence thinkers

have exercised their ingenuity to discover
whether exceptions could be made to this
or that law of nature, the laws of motion
or the law of the conservation of energy,
while preserving the rest of the order of
nature intact. It has been enquired into
whether the equations of physical happening have any indeterminate roots, so that,
like a man at the North Pole who must go
south if he goes anywhere on the surface,
and who may go south in a million different ways, the event requires some deciding
factor from outside the physical situation
to rescue it from a complete physical in-
ability to decide.

We must consider these enquiries, but
we must also view them with a degree of
distrust: the problem of freedom will not
be solved by the kind of ingenuity which
makes the successful inventor. For the order of the world is not cunning: its secrets
are not a game of wit set for the witty.
There can, of course, be no mechanical explanation of freedom: to explain it caus-
ally would be to deny it. Nor does freedom occur as an exceptional event, through
an interference in the laws of nature by a

non-natural agent. It is the whole self that is free, not a fraction of it; and there is no clash of laws in the case. We cannot understand freedom by way of physics or chemistry, nor in spite of physics and chemistry; but we are still bound to enquire how, or whether, in view of the truth of physics and chemistry, freedom is possible.

BUT if physical laws are not set aside, nor interfered with, how can there be any indeterminism? An answer may be discerned in the familiar notion of the relativity of laws. Any physical law is relative when it is a special case of a more general law, and as a special case has a restricted field of validity. Thus the law of the expansion of bodies by heat is relatively true; but it is a consequence of the more general law of intermolecular motion, and this more general law explains exceptions to the more special law, as that ice in melting does not expand. The physicist is well accustomed to operate with laws which are only relatively true. In fact, all laws are relative *except the one law* from which they are all derived. What is that one law?

Is it Einstein's generalization? Probably not. If there is any ultimate physical law it must be stated as a law of the behavior of the ultimate physical units. Laws of the behavior of atoms are more nearly final than laws of the behavior of molecules; for they include the laws by which molecules are built and broken as well as the law which the molecules as atom-complexes follow. What, then, if there *are no ultimate physical units?* If the atom gives way to the electron, shall the electron or the proton be the last outpost of nature's subtlety because it stands at the limit of our present powers of analysis? Physics will not be dogmatic here. Beyond each new stage of penetration into nature's detail, it will surmise other stages. And if there is no assignable limit to the analysis of the physical event, there is no physical law which can assume to be *the* law of change.

The physicist is never dealing with *the law* of the world, and never needs to. He can never be sure that he has found that law, because he can never be sure that he has reached the last analysis of the physi-

cal object. It remains open to us, then, to
say what we know of the law of happening
as we find it in ourselves. Here, it is a *law
of meaning*. Things happen because of
what they mean to us; and as our meanings
grow, things take different courses. The
outer and inner views of freedom cannot
remain in splendid isolation: they are views
of the same thing, and that thing is the
pursuit and realization of value.

The laws of physical nature are relative
to the law of meaning; and so far as meanings do not change, these relative laws may
be treated as absolute. Nature is a realm of
common and steadfast ingredients of will:
its reliableness is implied in the law of
meaning. The steadfastness of the known
laws of nature, so far as they apply to
existing situations, is not at all incompati-
ble with the utmost liberty of change, so
far as they do not apply!

Thus, the body as a thing of nature
shows me my dependence on heredity and
environment, my law of growth and decline, my fate, my certainty of death. Let
it do so. This is what it must do as a faithful drawer of consequences. Unless it did

this with complete fidelity it would be a
worthless servant, like an erratic watch. So
far as the body is immersed in the natural
order, it presents me a stream of well-ad-
justed events which afford me certain data
for action. These data fit into their subordinate places in the hierarchy of action
whose total result is directed simply from
the seat of conscious will.

BUT what happens in the brain while the
self is living? I do not know—I can only
guess. But there are certain things we do
know about the course of mental events
which supply material for conjecture, more
or less reasonable. Shall we indulge in a
brief excursion of speculation?

We know that there is such a thing as
mental energy, and that it varies in some
respects with general physical energy,
while in other respects it seems to vary independently. Mental energy is not mani-
fested always in measurable exertion. It
is rather shown in *poise*. It acts, as Lao
Tze said long ago, by non-assertion. Mental power is measured by range of vision;
and the range of vision is greatest when

contending impulses are held in equipoise,
while the self considers which impulse shall
become the bearer of its meaning. Thus,
when I am balancing between a present enjoyment and a future satisfaction the conscious time-field becomes extended. Mental energy is proportionate to the silent
and physically effortless grasp of thought.
The characteristic effort of the self in reflexion is the effort to conceive this or that
course of action as promoting its hope,
that is, as providing a transition from what
it is to what it prefers to be. It is at least
conceivable that in such effort a physical
aspect of energy is enhanced, that we are
creating potential energy in acquiring
equilibrium, and that we have in the brain
a spring or a sink through which fluxes of
this quantity take place.

We know, further, that in reflexion the
self alters its relation to the time-series of
physical events. Reflexion, as an act of
self-awareness, has its own date; but having taken place, it makes an object of that
time-series, and occupies a position having
a certain independence of time-rate. The
brain-events, and the "stream of conscious-

ness" corresponding to them have their own rate of flow. If the self were a fixed function of this stream, its "decisions" would be borne along as inevitably as the oarless boat in a current. But, as aware of that stream, the self is not borne along by it, nor are its decisions. It is not hurried on by that physically established rate of change, but hovers over it as it were in a distinct time-series: its decisions are issued in its own time as its own decisions.

Now it is at least conceivable in a world in which space and time are to some extent functions of one another, that any control of the time-relations of events carries with it a control—it matters not how minute— of their space-relations. It is conceivable that in the direction toward the future there lies before the self not space-one-and-absolute but a certain space-variety or space-spread, which the movement of life continuously reduces to singleness, and that this reduction is the essential business of life in the natural world. If this reduc-tion were accompanied by variations in the available energy of the brain centers, as suggested above, it would be what we

should physically expect. The time-free-
dom of the self would be seen as the original ingredient in its concrete physical freedom.

IN their full development, the lines of action between which I am choosing may be
widely different—a hunting trip to Pata-
gonia or a conference of philosophers in
Rangoon—and they will be represented
by widely different patterns in my neural
set. But the immediate issue is not concerned with this broad diversity: it is concerned with differences of worth in the
several possibilities, and perhaps with differences in *kind* of worth. There may be
at stake an increase of political power and
a loss of the finer edge of honor. The issue
is, at last, what kind of world do I choose
to live in? For this is what decides the kind
of value that is achievable and important.
I hold *this* possibility before my eyes, and
see this course, x, as the way to it: I hold
that possibility in view, and see this other
way, y, as the way to it. The way I turn
depends on the vivid realism with which
one or other kind of good presents itself.

My *belief* turns the scale of action: and the effort of decision is an effort to see clearly enough to shape the cast of belief.

On the physical side, if it were observable, this inner change which marks decision would show itself as a growing flush of activity in one of the waiting sets of action. It begins as an insensible change, a passage from zero to something, like the passage from a tangent into a curve or the fall of a rain drop on one side or other of a watershed. The physical issue lies in a physically indiscoverable alternative at the peak of the hierarchy of conditions of change. And my conjecture is that we have, at every instant of our lives, the choice before us which of several closely-related future space-time-worlds shall become the continuous prolongation of the past-and-present space-time-world.

These are speculations: let it be with them as it may. The enquiry is one for the physicist, the biologist, and the philosopher to work out in coöperation. In any case, freedom is the given fact. Nature, as world of law, is a subordinate and partly hypo-

thetical fact, and must adjust its theories
to our primary datum.

12. DEGREES OF FREEDOM

The nature of freedom will be clearer to
us if we remember that freedom is a matter of degree.

Freedom runs down daily. We are more
mechanical at the end of a day's work than
at the beginning. We make more mistakes
in our thinking and behaving. Fatigue,
strained attention, hunger—a hundred
causes limit our elasticity, restrict the
range of our vision, block our access to
more liberal alternatives of mood and
meaning. We approach the condition of a
mechanical manikin.

At its limit, freedom might be considered as reduced to zero. With its disappearance, conscious direction would vanish
also. Habit might be regarded as operating
the machine without the intrusion of living
interest. There are abnormal states of
human nature which suggest such a picture. "Asylums are full of pitiful economic
persons who, lost to the laws of social life,
continue as automatons to follow an un-

modified instinct in picking up and hoarding pins, leaves, scraps of food, paper."* We are all aware of bordering at times on some similar stage of unfreedom, as when our very smiles, in a long-drawn-out social function, become mechanical responses-to-stimuli, uncharged with the personal perceptions whose fountain has run dry.

When freedom is at zero, the self is perfectly inserted in nature. The cycle of causation is complete; its original impulses come wholly from the outer mechanisms of the world. If the mind awakes, meaning begins to have a share in directing the course of events, and events are different because of this direction. The cycle still remains complete, and no external observer can detect the fact that the self is no longer perfect in its insertion. But a subtle change has taken place in the sources of motion: energy is being sent into the circuit, as it were, through its pores. The self is holding before itself now an object-good which is its own, not a mere projection of the results of nature and habit: reason, instead of being controlled by impulse, or pas-

* Carleton H. Parker, *Motives in Economic Life.*

sively lending itself to "rationalize" an irrational motive-force, is building the *meaning* of every impulse or passion into the body of its hope; and the courses of outgoing action are being turned into channels in which they promise to promote that hope.

The degree of freedom is measured by the liveliness of that hope, the unstraining tension of the self toward it, and the consequent irradiation of the several activities of the self by that will-object. Whatever renews one's effortless grasp of his hope— such as rest, play, worship—increases the degree of freedom. Worship may be described as the deliberate effort to restore or increase freedom by renewing the relation of the self to its ultimate hope.*

Our ultimate freedom lies in the fact that we are free to control the degree of our freedom, through these various natural arts of recreation. The last crime against our own natures is the choice, itself a free choice, to drift into that state of helpless

* This view is developed in an article by the author, "The Illicit Naturalizing of Religion," in *The Journal of Religion,* November, 1923.

control by habit and impulse in which it becomes literally true that we "have no choice."

THE degrees of our freedom are the degrees of our own reality. We are free in proportion as we see things as they are, and ourselves as they are. We may say, if we like, that we are free in proportion as we are rational and reflective; but we ought also to say that we are free in proportion as we respect the *instinct* that is in us. For instinct, properly understood, is a hold on reality; it is anything but a mechanical affair; it makes for the increase of freedom. Here we encounter some of the outstanding mysteries of psychology for the nature-bound view of mind.

What is this impulse sometimes called the "instinct of workmanship"? Not an instinct, of course, in the technical sense—more like a dominant passion in some men: but a verifiable trait in most men, under whatever name. A carpenter earning high wages tells me he is dissatisfied because he is hurried in his work: "a man never gets a chance to do his best." Why does he want

a chance to do his best—he will earn no
more by it? Or what is it that keeps the
business man going when he has heaped up
all he can use? Not greed. Not ambition
exactly. Something more like a modified
instinct of workmanship. There is something *there to be done:* it seems to him that
he must be the one to do it. What is it that
makes a good housekeeper, or a good captain of a ship? Something that exceeds
every definable duty. The officer who
studied instructions and fulfilled them all
would never, on that ground, become the
captain of a ship. The man who becomes
captain is the man who finds his orders in
the ship itself and its mission, and who does
whatever at any time there is no one else
to do. The work of the ship is his work:
something objective, something not in him
is issuing requirements, and he is there to
fulfil them. To a sound instinct it is never
a particular stimulus alone, *it is reality
that commands.* The living instinct of man
has in it an element of the mystical: it is
responding to the world in its invisible
unity.

It is not human instinct alone that

looks thus beyond its physical stimulus. Throughout the animal kingdom, the maternal instinct shows this sense of being. A correspondent sends me a plea for retaining the word "divine" as descriptive of this quality in the animal world, while abolishing the idea of God as its object. "To change the name of the abysmal mystery need not abolish mysticism. It might almost seem to plunge the mind into deeper mystery, and an added sense of the tragic sublimity of the principle in the hen, the monkey, the tigress, which in order that the race may go on at all has been stuffed into animal life by nature. The reference to God only obscures what we can see clearly enough, that this element is sacrificial and pure, that is, goodness." I agree with my correspondent that the maternal instinct in animals, as in the little monkey that Darwin tells about, frequently shows the genuine beauty of devotion. I am willing to say that in the animal response to the total demand of life we can see the germ of religion. But in man, instinct becomes self-conscious and self-critical, and can survive only if, with all his science, he

can still approve its object. It is man's
business to know what his impulses mean:
and hence if there is any impulse in animal
or man that deserves the name "divine,"
it is because the reality to which his instinct is responding is a reasonable object
of loyalty.

Thus, in our view of what the *world is,*
in our metaphysical creed the freedom of
man is at stake. For freedom can live but
precariously on a self-sustained hope—a
courageous will-to-hope in a world which
may be a scaffold to all human hope. Courage in such a world seems almost a mis-
nomer, a dramatic concealment of disaffec-
tion and dismay which would better make
common cause in meeting with all due wisdom, pride, and grace the approaching
darkness. Freedom can grow great only as
hope can find its possible good an object
of genuine belief. Hence the life of freedom depends intimately on the validity of
the mystic's worship.

ONE more conclusion may be drawn. The
bodily life of the self is a life in space and
time, in one particular space-time order,

that which pertains to this world of nature. The self needs a body, we say, in order to be itself; it needs a world of nature in order that it may have a body. Then, without a body, and a relation to nature, no self. With the death of the body, the self must cease to exist; unless, indeed, there may be for it another body and another nature. In this world of nature, there can be for it no other body; can there be any other world of nature? Has the word "other" in this connection any tangible meaning?

There is, of course, the space of dream, of imagination, of the artist's fabric; and with these spaces there arise new and other worlds of nature. But they are not "real." *This* space and its contents we distinguish as real, the space of scientific fact, the space to which I return when I cease dreaming and imagining. We call it real, in part, because it is "our" space, the space of our mutual conversation: its reality is borne in to us from outside, we receive it; it is the original of all our dreams.

But meantime, is the self not also "real"? Can anything be more real than this pres-

ent awareness, sensitive to pleasure and
pain. Have I a right to exclude from my
inventory of real things the suffering I
cause or the resentment I provoke? If I
forget them they will make themselves felt
and maintain thereby that the self and its
states of feeling are co-real with the rocks
and atoms. And with this reality of the
self does there not go a degree of reality
in its products? The creative capacity of
the self is a real capacity; and its products
are not zeros in the universe of real things.
What shall we say, then, of the spaces,
worlds, bodies, to which in its creative imagining it gives birth?

We have to say that they are not *intended* to be real, or more accurately, they
are not intended by their authors to knit
in with *this* world of nature which we agree
to call the real world. Intention has something to do with the designation of the real
order; it may be to a greater degree than
we think that the accent of reality is con-
ferred upon nature by the selves which
participate in it. For if reality can emanate from any self, it may emanate in some
degree from every self: and it is not be-

yond doubt whether nature taken by itself can maintain the quality of reality. In
proportion as the world with which physics
deals, as it penetrates to the kernel of nature's being, resolves into a play of quality-
less mathematical terms and equations, it
begins to appear that physics on its own
ground has nothing wherewith to distinguish between the real and the unreal.*
Reality is not a physical property: the
solidity and impenetrability of former
days have gone. The grounds on which
we return to *this* space-time order, as the
existent in a privileged sense, appear to be
of a social or super-physical character. The
self in the exercise of its freedom looks into
a world of imagination, another space-time
order, but with an intention different from
that of the dream: its intention is that this
other world shall *become* real, and it does
so. Is this reality-conferring power restricted to what is woven in with this present course of nature?

That appears to me improbable. The
self stands as the vinculum between a plu-

* See Eddington in *Science, Religion and Reality,*
edited by Joseph Needham, p. 211.

rality of space-time orders: it is not completely absorbed in any one of them; and
no one of them is for it exclusively real.
But one of them is exclusively its *present
business;* for it is the space-time of this
body and of this group of associates. Let
us suppose that this group is not the sole
group of selves in the universe. Then the
death of this body, which would certainly
mean the severing of connection with this
present group of selves, need not mean the
cessation of all relation between the affected self and other selves. Such death is
not *ipso facto* the extinction either of the
space-and-world-creating powers which
that self, in its receptive apprenticeship,
has developed, nor of that principle of
growth which determines it to a pursuit of
concrete value in common with other selves.
With other such groups it may conceivably
entertain another body and another field
of nature. Unless in its use of freedom a
self has freely resigned freedom and made
itself "a part of nature and not something
in contrast to nature" there is no presumption, scientific or otherwise, that *this* nature must circumscribe its destiny.

The life of the unsatisfied self, whose importance the contemporary psychologist has discovered, and before him, Schopenhauer, and before Schopenhauer, Hegel and Augustine, Plato and Paul, Buddha, and Lao Tze, is the best assurance that in the hidden arrangements of the universe this persistent flame, half choked and fitful in the present order, may continue its quest of breath and freedom in another.